THE NOBLE ART OF
HEAVYWEIGHT
BOXING

THE NOBLE ART OF HEAVYWEIGHT BOXING

★ RALPH OATES ★

ROBERT HALE • LONDON

ISBN 978-0-7198-1743-4

Robert Hale Limited
Clerkenwell House
Clerkenwell Green
London EC1R 0HT

www.halebooks.com

A catalogue record for this book is available from the British Library

2 4 6 8 10 9 7 5 3 1

Designed by Dave Jones
Printed by Craft Print International Ltd, Singapore

Dedicated to the memory of Ruby Oates,
who was a very special lady

Contents

Foreword

I was pleased when Ralph Oates asked me to write a foreword for his book, *The Noble Art of Heavyweight Boxing*. I had no doubt that his latest publication would provide the many fans of the sport with a number of interesting facts about the weight division. Indeed, Ralph has presented many items of interest about the heavyweights in an easy-to-follow way, which makes the book a joy to read, whether in your home or on a train.

For a number of years I fought in both the amateur and professional ranks at heavyweight, winning the Amateur Boxing Association (ABA) title in 1961 and, when as a professional, challenging for the British, European and Commonwealth titles at heavyweight. Along the way I fought men like Henry Cooper, Karl Mildenberger, Johnny Prescott, Thad Spencer, Eduardo Corletti, Joe Erskine, Brian London, Joe Bygraves, Ray Patterson, Giulio Rinaldi and Jack Bodell – all good fighters. So Ralph's book holds a special interest for me. Over the years Ralph has served fight fans well, having been a former amateur boxer himself and having written a number of well-received books on the sport.

For almost three years Ralph had his own boxing column for a local newspaper and was a contributor to *The British Boxing Board of Control Boxing Yearbook*. He is also the former Boxing Consultant for *The Guinness Book of Records*, so you can be sure he knows his subject.

Ralph is, of course, well known for his quiz books. In *The Noble Art of Heavyweight Boxing* Ralph has come up with something a little different, but still you get the feeling that you are discovering something new or refreshing your memory about past events that you may well have forgotten about – or even historical events which may not have occurred to you at the time! There is little doubt in my mind if you are a boxing fan you will enjoy *The Noble Art of Heavyweight Boxing* as it packs a knockout punch of heavyweight proportions in the knowledge department of the sport, that's for sure. So go to your corners and come out reading!

Billy Walker, BRITISH BOXING BOARD OF CONTROL ADMINISTRATOR AND FORMER
EUROPEAN, BRITISH AND COMMONWEALTH HEAVYWEIGHT CONTENDER

Introduction

I don't think anyone would really disagree with the statement that, in boxing, it's the heavyweight poundage which dominates the sport. Whenever a prospect emerges in the division, the eyes of the boxing world will follow his progress with keen interest. Very often the new hope will appear to attract more publicity than a more talented boxer who fights in a lighter division.

This may seem an injustice to the lighter man – and, in truth, it very often is – but such a fact is evidence that it's the big men who have the appeal. There are, of course, exceptions to the rule, but a young heavyweight who is considered to have real potential is pure gold dust at the box office. The show often sells a great deal of tickets when said boxer is fighting, much to the promoter's delight.

The ultimate goal of any heavyweight with genuine talent is to fight for and win the world championship – a title which, without doubt, is the most revered in boxing and perhaps the whole sporting world in general. The heavyweight championship, like all items of value, is difficult to obtain; only the talented, and perhaps a few fighters with luck on their side, are able to wear the prized crown. In fact, until recent years very few Europeans had success when challenging for the championship.

The American heavyweights were number one, clearly superior in every way. There was, of course, the occasional blip when a fighter from outside the USA had been able to win the championship (or a version of it), and when it happened it was BIG news. However, it did not last long; the title was soon back in the land of 'stars and stripes'. In fact, the heavyweight championship had been won so many times by Americans that it was once considered to be the rightful property of the USA.

These days the situation is dramatically different, with fighters from other parts of the world regularly winning the crown. With different versions of the title up for grabs, due to the existence of rival boxing organizations, the task of winning a world crown would seem (to the casual follower of the sport, at least) much easier than it once was. But make no mistake: that is not always the case. In truth, contesting any one of the championships is extremely difficult, even a minor version of the crown.

After all, a championship is a championship, and a win takes the respective fighter to another level, which in turn means a bigger purse next time out when defending the crown. Retaining the title for any period of time is often an even bigger challenge than winning it in the first place. There are so many hungry fighters knocking on the championship door, eager to take over the throne. No champion can afford to be complacent.

On the subject of champions, let's not count out America completely. American boxers still figure highly when it comes to the battle inside the square ring. The Americans do not dominate the heavyweight category in the way they once did, but America does appear to turn out a vast number of heavyweight contenders on a conveyor-belt type of system, one after another, all of whom are a constant threat. Check the world rankings at any given time and you'll find a boxer from the USA on the verge of a title fight, ensuring the country will have a presence among the title-holders for many years to come. There is every chance that the USA will produce another man, in the not-too-distant future, who will dominate the weight division in much the same way as Muhammad Ali, Joe Louis, and Rocky Marciano once did.

The heavyweight crown has been worn by some very fine fighters over the years, many of whom can be considered great, or will be considered great with the passing of time. Men such as the three mentioned above, along with Jack Dempsey, Floyd Patterson, Larry Holmes, Joe Frazier, Mike Tyson, Evander Holyfield and Lennox Lewis. There are of course many other potential greats, who have graced the championship with skill, pride and dignity, and who, on their respective nights, have given the fans something to think about (and hence, talk about) for a very long time.

Boxing needs good heavyweights to stimulate the game; an exciting champion at the weight will always attract public interest and vast attention from the media, which in turn helps the sport to maintain its popularity, and this is vital for the health of the sport. Will we ever see another fighter with the vast skills and the drawing power of Muhammad Ali? Will we ever again admire the fearful aggression and attacking styles of Mike Tyson and Joe Frazier, or the consummate skills of Lennox Lewis? We can but hope. *The Noble Art of Heavyweight Boxing* is based on just some of the fascinating aspects of the heavyweight division I've observed over the years, be it in the ring or by association. I do hope you enjoy reading about them.

Ralph Oates

★ ★ ★ ACKNOWLEDGEMENTS ★ ★ ★

My thanks to Howard Oates
for his assistance in checking
the facts for this book.

Also for the support of my family
Denise, David, Colin and Victoria Oates,
along with Charlotte and Sam Webb.

I wish to thank the following people
for their kind permission in allowing me
to reproduce their photographs: Les Clark,
Tania Follett, Derek Rowe and Philip Sharkey.

Finally, my thanks to Dave Jones,
Gill Jackson and Lavinia Porter
for their help in producing this book

WORLD BOXING ORGANIZATIONS

EBU	European Boxing Union
IBF	International Boxing Federation
IBO	International Boxing Organization
NBA	National Boxing Association
NABF	North American Boxing Federation
NY	New York
UBA	Universal Boxing Association
WBA	World Boxing Association
WBC	World Boxing Council
WBF	World Boxing Federation
WBO	World Boxing Organization
WBU	World Boxing Union

WORLD BOXING ORGANIZATIONS

CHAPTER ONE

FROM BAREKNUCKLES TO MARQUESS OF QUEENSBERRY RULES

The last bareknuckle contest for the world heavyweight title took place on 8 July 1889 in Richburg, USA, between defending champion John L. Sullivan and challenger Jake Kilrain. Anyone expecting to get home early would have been disappointed since the bout last a reported two and a half hours, with Sullivan finally retaining his crown with a stoppage in the *seventy-fifth* round!

The first world heavyweight title fight fought under the Marquess of Queensberry rules took place on 7 September 1892 between John L. Sullivan and James J. Corbett. The contest, which pitted the scientific boxing skills of Corbett against the hard-hitting Sullivan, was held in New Orleans, USA. Corbett knocked out Sullivan in the twenty-first round to win the championship.

Charlie Mitchell became the first British boxer to challenge for the world heavyweight championship under Marquess of Queensberry rules on 25 January 1894 when he met holder James J. Corbett in Jacksonville, USA. The efforts of Mitchell proved to be in vain when he was counted out in the third round.

Champion John L. Sullivan won the last bareknuckle contest for the world heavyweight title

Bob Fitzsimmons fought Tom Sharkey in a contest which took place in San Francisco on 2 December 1896. Sharkey won the encounter when Fitzsimmons was disqualified in round eight for an alleged low blow. The decision was most controversial since there were many who did not agree with the referee's action. However, few, if any, were prepared to take issue with this decision as the referee in question was none other than the legendary Wyatt Earp, the US Marshal famous for the gunfight at the OK Corral. Clearly, this referee was not a man to argue with!

The first British-born boxer to win the world heavyweight crown was Bob Fitzsimmons, who knocked out defending champion James J. Corbett in round fourteen with a left to the solar plexus.

The contest, which took place on 17 March 1897 in Carson City, USA, gave Fitzsimmons the distinction of being the first former world middleweight champion to win this title.

The event also marked the first occasion a world heavyweight title contest was filmed.

James J. Jeffries won the world heavyweight title on 9 June 1899 when he knocked out defending champion Bob Fitzsimmons in round eleven. The contest took place at Coney Island, New York.

In winning the title, Jeffries helped his manager, William A. Brady, to contribute to the pages of boxing history by becoming the first man to manage *two* world heavyweight champions (Brady had previously taken James J. Corbett to the title in 1892).

Bob Fitzsimmons became the first British-born boxer to win the world heavyweight title on 17 March 1897 when he knocked out the title-holder James J. Corbett

On 3 November 1899 James J. Jeffries retained his world heavyweight title at Coney Island in New York, outpointing opponent Tom Sharkey over the duration of twenty-five rounds. This was the first time that a world championship fight in the heavyweight division had gone the full distance.

When Tom Sharkey challenged James J. Jeffries for the title in 1899, he became the first Irish-born boxer to challenge for the world heavyweight championship. Sharkey was born in Dundalk, Ireland.

On 6 April 1900 James J. Jeffries knocked out challenger Jack Finnegan in round one when defending his world heavyweight title in Detroit, USA. The contest lasted for just fifty-five seconds – a case of 'if you blinked, you missed it'!

Jeffries created the record of having achieved the then fastest win on record in a world heavyweight title fight.

Owing to Jeffries' speedy finish, the 1900 Jeffries–Finnegan contest was the first world heavyweight title fight to finish in the first round.

American George Siler was the referee of the Jeffries–Finnegan title fight and thus became the first person to referee four consecutive world heavyweight title fights, the previous three for which he was referee being:

★   Bob Fitzsimmons v. James J. Corbett (1897)
★   James J. Jefferies v. Bob Fitzsimmons (1899)
★   James J. Jefferies v. Tom Sharkey (1899)

James J. Corbett became champion in the first title bout under the Marquess of Queensberry rules

On 11 May 1900 James J. Corbett became the first fighter to try to regain the world heavyweight title when he challenged champion James J. Jeffries at Coney Island, New York. Corbett, however, failed in his attempt when Jeffries, who was making a third defence of his championship title, knocked him out in round twenty-three.

Bob Fitzsimmons became the second fighter to attempt to regain the world heavyweight title when he challenged James J. Jeffries in San Francisco, USA, on 25 July 1902. However, Jeffries retained the crown, knocking out Fitzsimmons in round eight.

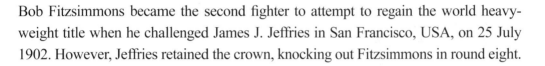

Clearly James J. Corbett had not given up any hopes of once again ruling the heavyweight division when, on 14 August 1903, he became the first man to make two attempts at regaining the world heavyweight championship in San Francisco, USA. However, defending title-holder James J. Jefferies retained the crown when Corbett, whose corner had thrown in the towel to stop him taking punishment, retired in round ten.

On 25 November 1903 Bob Fitzsimmons captured the world light-heavyweight crown when he outpointed defending champion, Irish-born George Gardner, over twenty rounds in San Francisco, USA. In doing so, Fitzsimmons became the first former world heavyweight champion to move down a weight division and thus win the title.

As a result of his defeat of Gardner in 1903, Fitzsimmons also became the first man in boxing to win a championship in *three* weight divisions, having also been a world champion at middleweight!

The American Sam Berger became the first man to win an Olympic gold medal at heavyweight when he defeated fellow American Charles Meyer at the 1904 Games, held in St Louis, USA.

On 28 March 1905 Marvin Hart outpointed opponent Jack Johnson over twenty rounds in San Francisco, USA. However, Johnson would win the championship three years later in 1908.

When James J. Jeffries retired from boxing, Marvin Hart and Jack Root contested the vacant crown. The pair met in Reno, USA, on 3 July 1905, and Hart duly became the new champion when he knocked out his opponent in round twelve.

The referee of the match was the retired former champion James J. Jeffries, who therefore became the first ever former world heavyweight title-holder to referee a world heavyweight title bout.

On 23 February 1906 the world heavyweight championship was brought down low when Canadian Tommy Burns won the title by outpointing American holder Marvin Hart over twenty rounds in Los Angeles, USA. This was not due to any form of indiscretion on the part of the new champion; it was simply his height. Standing at just 5 ft 7 in., Burns became the shortest man in the history of the sport to hold the heavyweight championship.

When Tommy Burns captured the championship from Marvin Hart in 1906, it marked the very first occasion for the world heavyweight title to change hands by way of a points decision.

On 28 November 1906 Tommy Burns made the second defence of his title against 'Philadelphia' Jack O'Brien in Los Angeles, USA. After twenty rounds the points were even and so Burns retained his crown by way of a draw.

This was the first time that a drawn verdict had been given in a world heavyweight title fight.

On 2 December 1907 Canadian Tommy Burns defended his world heavyweight title against Briton Gunner Moir in London. British hopes of having their first world champion at the weight since Bob Fitzsimmons were duly dashed when Burns retained his championship by knocking out Moir in round ten.

This was the first world heavyweight title fight to be staged in Britain and the first to take place outside the USA.

It was a case of 'Rule Britannia' when the 1908 Olympic Games took place in London. The gold medal in the heavyweight division went to the host nation's A.L. Oldham, who put his name in the record books as Britain's very first heavyweight champion in this event.

On 17 March 1908 Ireland had its first world heavyweight title fight in Dublin. However, defending champion Tommy Burns made short work of the task, knocking out Irish challenger Jem Roche in the first round. The contest took just eighty-eight seconds, making it, at the time, the second fastest win in the history of world title bouts in the division.

France was treated to two world heavyweight title fights in 1908. The first ever championship contest to be staged at the weight in this European country took place on 18 April in Paris, where holder Tommy Burns found the punches to knock out British challenger Jewey Smith in the fifth round. On 13 June – again in the French capital – Burns knocked out Australian challenger Bill Squires in round eight.

Squires had previously challenged Burns in America on 4 July 1907, but on that occasion he had met with defeat after being counted out in the first round.

Next stop for the travelling Tommy Burns was Sydney, Australia, where, on 24 August 1908, he gave Australians their first-ever world heavyweight title fight. In the challenger's corner was Bill Squires, a man who had already challenged Burns twice for the crown. However, it was not going to be third time lucky for Squires, who once again tasted defeat when knocked out in round thirteen by Burns.

In 1908 the first black fighter to win the world heavyweight championship was Jack Johnson, who stopped defending title-holder Tommy Burns in round fourteen. Burns, who was making the twelfth defence of his championship in Sydney, Australia, found that he was no match for the big, talented American.

In 1908 Jack Johnson became the first black boxer to win the world heavyweight crown when he defeated Tommy Burns ... on Boxing Day!

At the time of his defeat to Jack Johnson, Tommy Burns had now participated in thirteen world heavyweight title bouts. Burns had thus created a record, since he had now taken part in more world heavyweight title fights than any other boxer in the division at that time.

The list opposite shows the number of title defences Burns made prior to and at the time of his defeat to Johnson.

Prior to his defeat by Jack Johnson in 1908, Tommy Burns had created another record in the heavyweight division, having successfully stopped eight consecutive challengers inside the scheduled distance in title defences.

On 10 March 1909 world heavyweight champion Jack Johnson fought a six-round exhibition with a man who went on to become a well-known Hollywood actor, Victor McLaglen. One of the many films McLaglen appeared in during his career was *The Informer*, for which he won an Academy Award. McLaglen also had a major role in *The Quiet Man*, in which he was involved in a very long and comical fight scene with the star John Wayne.

On 1 June 1913 Georges Carpentier became the first French boxer to win the European heavyweight title when he knocked out Briton Bombardier Billy Wells in round four in a bout that took place in Belgium.

★ ★ ★ NUMBER OF TITLE DEFENCES FOR ★ ★ ★

★ TOMMY BURNS ★

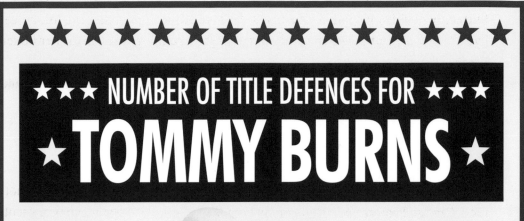

OPPONENT	RESULT FOR BURNS	DATE
Marvin Hart	won on points over 20 rounds (won title)	23 Feb 1906
Jim Flynn	won knockout in fifteenth round	2 Oct 1906
Philadelphia Jack O'Brien	drew over 20 rounds	28 Nov 1906
Philadelphia Jack O'Brien	won on points over 20 rounds	8 May 1907
Bill Squires	won knockout in first round	4 Jul 1907
Gunner Moir	won knockout in tenth round	2 Dec 1907
Jack Palmer	won knockout in fourth round	10 Feb 1908
Jem Roche	won knockout in first round	17 Mar 1908
Jewey Smith	won knockout in fifth round	18 Apr 1908
Bill Squires	won knockout in eighth round	13 Jun 1908
Bill Squires	won knockout in thirteenth round	24 Aug 1908
Bill Lang	won knockout in sixth round	2 Sep 1908
Jack Johnson	lost stopped in fourteenth round	26 Dec 1908

On 19 December 1913 Jack Johnson defended his crown against American challenger Jim Johnson in Paris, France. The bout was declared a draw after ten rounds. While not exactly an explosive encounter, the fight made history because it was the first time that two black fighters had stepped into the ring to face each other for the world heavyweight championship.

Despite the coincidence of sharing the same surname, the two fighters were not related.

On 27 June 1914 Jack Johnson made yet another defence of his world heavyweight title in Paris, France. This time his challenger was fellow American Frank Moran, who lost a twenty-round points decision in Johnson's favour.

The referee of this contest was none other than Georges Carpentier of France, the then reigning European champion at the weight and also a potential contender for Johnson's own title. Carpentier, therefore, had a close-up view of the boxing skills possessed by Johnson. However, during the course of their respective careers Johnson and Carpentier never crossed gloves in the ring.

Jess Willard won the world heavyweight title on 5 April 1915 in Havana, Cuba, when he knocked out defending champion Jack Johnson in round twenty-six. In doing so Willard became, at that time, the tallest man in the history of the division to hold the heavyweight crown, standing at the listed height of 6 ft 6½ in.

The contest was the very first world heavyweight title contest to be staged in Cuba.

In 1915 the fight between Willard and Johnson was held in Cuba – the very first heavyweight title contest to be staged there. It also was the last world heavyweight title contest to be scheduled for forty-five rounds.

CHAPTER TWO

BETWEEN THE WARS

On 4 July 1919 Jack Dempsey won the world heavyweight title in Toledo, USA, when defending champion Jess Willard retired in round three. Willard thus became the first champion in the heavyweight division to lose his crown by a corner retirement.

The 1919 fight between Dempsey and Willard was also notable because for the first time in a world heavyweight championship contest, judges were called upon for a decision (Tex Rickard and Anthony Drexel Biddle being the judges in question).

British heavyweight boxing was boosted in the 1920 Olympic Games, which were held in Antwerp, Belgium, when Ronald Rawson punched his way to a gold medal.

On 19 November 1920 young Bob Fitzsimmons knocked out opponent Carl Danner in four rounds in a contest which took place in New Jersey, USA.

Young Bob was the son of former world heavyweight, light-heavyweight *and* middleweight champion Bob Fitzsimmons. While young Bob had a lengthy ring career from a recorded 1919–31, he was unable to emulate his father's boxing success. Truly, Fitzsimmons senior was a hard act to follow.

During his fight with Jack Dempsey, Jess Willard (pictured) was knocked down seven times in the first round, eventually retiring in the third

On 2 July 1921 Jack Dempsey defended his world heavyweight championship against the French world light-heavyweight king Georges Carpentier in Jersey City, USA, and retained his crown by scoring a four-round knockout. This bout proved to be a landmark in the world of boxing, since it was the first contest to attract a million-dollar gate.

The European heavyweight title found a new home on 20 May 1923, when Erminio Spalla outpointed Holland's Piet van der Veer over twenty rounds for the vacant crown in Rome. Spalla became the first Italian to hold this championship.

On 4 July 1923 Tommy Gibbons challenged Jack Dempsey for the world heavy-weight title in Shelby, Montana, USA. While Tommy may have lost a fifteen-round points decision, he had at least gained a measure of satisfaction by becoming the first man to go the distance with Dempsey in a title bout.

In the action-packed world heavyweight title bout that took place on 14 September 1923 in New York, defending champion Jack Dempsey retained his crown by knocking out Luis Angel Firpo of Argentina in two explosive rounds.

The bout may have been short-lived, but it set a record at the time for the number of knock-downs in any single round. In the first round Firpo was floored seven times and Dempsey twice (including Dempsey being knocked out of the ring onto the press tables!) before the bout was concluded in the following session.

While Luis Angel Firpo may have failed to win the world heavyweight crown in 1923, he did go into the record books as the first heavyweight from Argentina to challenge for the title.

On 22 September 1923 in Milan, Italy's defending title-holder Erminio Spalla kept hold of his European heavyweight title when his defence against Belgium's Jack Humbeek was declared a draw over twenty rounds. This was the first time that a European title bout had finished with a draw being given.

On 18 May 1926 Spain's Paulino Uzcudun outpointed defending champion Erminio Spalla of Italy over fifteen rounds in Barcelona, Spain, to win the European heavyweight title. Thus, Uzcudun became the first Spanish boxer to hold this crown.

On 23 September 1926 in Philadelphia, USA, Gene Tunney took the heavyweight crown from Jack Dempsey with a ten-round points decision.

Almost a year to the day of that fight, Tunney and Dempsey met again. This contest, held on 22 September 1927 in Chicago, USA, proved to be the most controversial.

In the early stages of their return bout Tunney looked as if he would repeat the victory over Dempsey without any difficulties. However, in round seven of the contest, Dempsey caught Tunney with a series of blows to the head which sent him crashing to the canvas. At this point Dempsey should have quickly retreated to a neutral corner, but failed to do so and wasted precious time because the referee Dave Barry refused to start the count. Eventually Dempsey did go to a neutral corner, but by this time fourteen seconds had passed.

This short delay proved to be a valuable bonus for Tunney since it gave him extra time to recover. Gene was thus able to beat the count once it was picked up and went on to outpoint Dempsey over ten rounds to retain the crown.

Had Dempsey retreated to a neutral corner when required, it's possible that Tunney may not have been able to beat the count. Even if he had, he may well have been in a weakened state and easy prey for the hard-hitting challenger. In this contest Jack Dempsey could have made boxing history by becoming the first man to regain the world heavyweight title, but it was not to be.

Gene Tunney retired from boxing while still holding the world heavyweight crown. Tunney made the second defence of his title against Tom Heeney in New York on 26 July 1928, and stopped him in round eleven.

Gene became the first man to retire while still holding the world title and thus not make a futile comeback at a later date.

True to say Tom Heeney did not become the first New Zealander to win the world heavyweight championship, but he did become the first man from that country to challenge for the title when he fought Gene Tunney in July 1928.

Pierre Charles became the first boxer from Belgium to win the European heavyweight title on 3 February 1929 when he outpointed German Ludwig Haymann over fifteen rounds for the vacant crown in Dortmund, Germany.

On 12 June 1930 Germany's Max Schmeling met Jack Sharkey of America for the vacant heavyweight title in New York. Schmeling won the world championship when Sharkey was disqualified in the fourth round for throwing a punch that landed low.

This was the first time in the history of the sport that a world heavyweight title fight had finished with a disqualification.

On 3 July 1931 in Cleveland, Ohio, Max Schmeling of Germany made a successful defence of his world heavyweight crown when he stopped American challenger Young Stribling in round fifteen. Thus, Schmeling became the first non-American to defend the championship in the USA since Canada's Tommy Burns, who had knocked out Bill Squires in the first round in Los Angeles on 4 July 1907.

Hein Müller became the first German holder of the European heavyweight crown when he outpointed the then holder Pierre Charles of Belgium over fifteen rounds in Berlin on 30 August 1931.

In a return contest on 21 June 1932, Jack Sharkey became the new world heavyweight king when he outpointed holder Max Schmeling over fifteen rounds in Long Island, New York. However, in his first defence of the title (also in Long Island, New York) on 29 June 1933, Sharkey lost his crown when he was knocked out in round six by challenger Primo Carnera. This was the first time an American heavyweight had defeated a European boxer to win the world title, only to lose it to another European (Schmeling being German and Carnera Italian).

Jack Petersen became the first Welsh boxer to win the British heavyweight crown at Wimbledon Stadium in London on 12 July 1932 when he knocked out defending champion Reggie Meen in the second round.

When Petersen defeated Meen on this occasion he scored a double since he also became the first British light-heavyweight title-holder to move up a division and thus capture the domestic heavyweight championship.

When Jack Petersen won the British heavyweight crown he became the first former ABA light-heavyweight champion to do so. Petersen won the ABA title in 1931.

On 22 October 1933 Primo Carnera of Italy defended his world heavyweight title against Spain's Paulino Uzcudun in Rome and retained his crown with a fifteen-round points decision. This was the first time that two European heavyweights had faced each other for the world championship.

The Carnera–Uzcudun world heavyweight title fight in 1933 created a record, since at the time it became the heaviest title bout in the history of the sport. Carnera weighed a reported 18 st 7½ lb and Uzcudun 16 st 5¼ lb.

The 1933 Carnera–Uzcudun encounter was the very first world heavyweight title contest to be staged in Italy.

Len Harvey was crowned the new British heavyweight champion when he outpointed defending title-holder Jack Petersen over fifteen rounds in a contest that took place in London on 30 November 1933. Harvey became just the second British light-heavyweight title-holder to win the title.

In Miami, Florida, the then greatest weight difference in any world heavyweight championship bout was recorded on 1 March 1934 when Primo Carnera made the second defence of his title against former world light-heavyweight king Tommy Loughran. At the weighing-in, Carnera was a reported weight of 19 st 4 lb and Loughran was 13 st 2 lb. Even at such a lesser weight, the smaller man did himself proud by pushing Carnera all the way, but the champion retained his crown with a fifteen-round points decision.

On 14 June 1934 challenger Max Baer relieved Primo Carnera of his world heavyweight title by way of an eleven-round stoppage at Long Island, New York. During the course of the contest, Carnera was on the canvas on twelve occasions, thus setting up, at that time, a record number of knock-downs registered against the defending champion during the course of a world heavyweight title fight.

Strange to say, but before they met in the ring for real, both Primo Carnera and Max Baer boxed each other in the 1933 Hollywood movie *The Prize Fighter and the Lady*, which starred Myrna Loy. To keep the boxing theme going, Jack Dempsey also appeared in the film.

On 4 July 1934 American Joe Louis made his professional debut in Chicago against Jack Kracken, who was sent for an early shower when the bout ended in the first round, Louis having quickly delivered the knockout blow. Louis was to go on to become one of the greats of the division.

When Max Baer made the first defence of his world heavyweight title in Long Island, New York, on 13 June 1935 against challenger James J. Braddock, he looked a good bet to keep his crown – but you should never bet on boxing. Baer, the clear favourite, suffered a fifteen-round points defeat, which was a massive shock to the boxing and sporting world at the time.

Clearly, James J. Braddock had better luck in the heavyweight division because he had previously challenged Tommy Loughran for the world light-heavyweight title in New York on 18 July 1929, losing a fifteen-round points decision.

Former world heavyweight champion Max Schmeling became the first man to defeat Joe Louis in the professional ranks when he knocked him out in round twelve on 19 June 1936 in New York. This shows that there's no such thing as a sure thing, since Louis had been the favourite to punch his way to yet another victory. At the time the result provided yet another shock to the world of boxing.

Ben Foord made his mark on 17 August 1936 when he became the first South African to hold the British heavyweight title. Foord stopped the defending title-holder Jack Petersen in three rounds at Tigers Ground, Leicester, when the Empire crown was also at stake. Foord was able to challenge for the British championship because he had lived in the UK long enough to meet the required residential qualifications.

Welshman Tommy Farr outpointed defending British and Empire heavyweight champion Ben Foord of South Africa over fifteen rounds on 15 March 1937 at the Harringay Arena, London. By boxing his way to victory, Farr became only the second Welsh heavyweight to hold these crowns.

On 22 June 1937 in a contest in Chicago, USA, Joe Louis knocked out defending title-holder James J. Braddock in eight rounds to win the world championship. In doing so, Louis became the first black fighter to hold the heavyweight title since Jack Johnson, who had lost the title in 1915.

Against all expectations, Britain's Tommy Farr gave Joe Louis a tough battle when challenging for the world heavyweight championship. The contest, which took place in New York on 30 August 1937, was hard-fought with no quarter given. Farr lost a fifteen-round points decision and thus became the first Welshman to challenge for this title.

If revenge is sweet then Joe Louis must have had a large jar of honey to hand on 22 June 1938 when, in New York, USA, he made his fourth defence of the title against the man who had given him his first defeat in the professional ranks, Max Schmeling.

From the sound of the first bell, Louis had gone hunting for his man, and he won when the towel was thrown in by Schmeling's corner in the first round, after only 124 seconds – at that time the third fastest win in a world heavyweight title fight.

On 25 January 1939 Joe Louis stopped former world light-heavyweight king John Henry Lewis in the first round in defence of his world heavyweight title, in a contest that took place in New York, USA. This was the first time that two black boxers had fought each other for the heavyweight crown since Jack Johnson and Jim Johnson in 1913.

On 17 April 1939 Joe Louis retained his world heavyweight title in Los Angeles, USA, by knocking out challenger Jack Roper in the first round. Louis thus became the first champion in the division to successfully retain his crown by halting three successive challengers in the opening round (Max Schmeling and John Henry Lewis being the previous two opponents to taste defeat in the first round).

On 20 September 1939 Joe Louis retained his world heavyweight title, knocking out challenger and fellow countryman Bob Pastor in round eleven. This was the first world heavyweight title contest to be staged in Detroit, USA, since April 1900, when James J. Jeffries knocked out Jack Finnegan in round one.

Arturo Godoy became the first boxer from Chile to challenge for the world heavyweight championship when he fought in New York on 9 February 1940. However, the defending title-holder, Joe Louis, retained his crown by a fifteen-round points decision.

On 17 December 1940 in New York Joe Baksi outpointed his opponent Jack Brazzo over four rounds. In the course of time Baksi went on to become a major player in the heavyweight division, but Brazzo's career took a very different direction.

Brazzo changed his name and went into acting, becoming one of Hollywood's leading stars, with films like *Shane*, *Panic in the Streets*, *Sudden Fear* and many more to his credit. He was nominated for three Academy Awards, winning an Academy Award for Best Supporting Actor in the 1991 movie *City Slickers*.

And what did Brazzo change his name to? Why, Jack Palance, of course!

On 21 March 1941 Joe Louis stopped challenger Abe Simon in thirteen rounds in defence of his championship in Detroit, USA. Had the contest lasted the full distance, it would have been a hard night for both fighters, since this was the last world heavyweight title contest to be scheduled for twenty rounds.

On 23 May 1941 Buddy Baer found a place in the record books when he became the first man to challenge for a world title formerly held by his brother, Max. The older Baer had duly held the world heavyweight championship from 1934–5. However, in 1941 Buddy failed to take the crown from defending title-holder Joe Louis in Washington DC when he was disqualified in round seven.

Joe Louis was one busy champion! He holds the record for successfully defending his world heavyweight crown more often in any one year than any other title-holder. Louis earned this distinction in 1941 when he defended his championship on *seven* occasions. That year his challengers were:

NUMBER OF TITLE DEFENCES FOR ★★★
★ JOE LOUIS ★
★★★ IN 1941 ★★★

OPPONENT	RESULT FOR JOE LOUIS	DATE
Red Burman	knocked out in five rounds	31 Jan
Gus Dorazio	knocked out in two rounds	17 Feb
Abe Simon	stopped in thirteen rounds	21 Mar
Tony Musto	stopped in nine rounds	8 Apr
Buddy Baer	disqualified in seven rounds	23 May
Billy Conn	knocked out in thirteen rounds	18 Jun
Lou Nova	stopped in six rounds	29 Sep

41

CHAPTER THREE

THE POST-WAR YEARS

On 12 May 1946 former world heavyweight champion Primo Carnera had his last professional contest in Gorizia, Italy, losing an eight-round points decision to fellow Italian Luigi Musina. During Carnera's successful career, he had a reported total of 103 bouts, winning eighty-eight and losing fourteen, with only one 'no contest'

However, at the time of his departure from the ring, Carnera held the record of winning more fights inside the distance (including two disqualification victories) than any other boxer who had held the heavyweight title – that number being an amazing *seventy-three*!

Bruce Woodcock can lay claim to being the first British heavyweight to be crowned European champion. Woodcock, the then reigning British and Empire heavyweight title-holder, met Frenchman Albert Renet at Belle Vue in Manchester, England, on 29 July 1946, and took the vacant championship when he knocked out his opponent in round six.

Until 1946 all European title fights were fought under the auspices of the International Boxing Union (IBU). In 1946 the IBU was renamed the European Boxing Union (EBU).

During his reign, world heavyweight champion Joe Louis proved to be a very active title-holder, and defended his crown on twenty-five occasions. This is a record for the division.

Joe Louis created yet another record by holding the world heavyweight championship for the longest length of time: from 22 June 1937 to 1 March 1949. The hiatus in competition was down to the fact that Louis served in the US army during his title reign, so as a professional boxer he was inactive in 1943, but was able to box in exhibition bouts during 1944–5 before returning to the professional ring in 1946.

Rocky Marciano, the 'Brockton Blockbuster', won his first professional contest on 17 March 1947, knocking out opponent Lee Epperson in three rounds in Holyoke, Massachusetts, USA.

Rocky Marciano continued to show that he was a fighter who did not like to hang around too long in the ring, halting his opponents before the final bell rang. Going in against opponent Don Mogard, Rocky had now won all his previous sixteen bouts inside the distance. In truth there was no reason to believe that the contest on 23 May 1949 in Providence would go the full scheduled route. Mogard, however, was able to rise to the occasion and, while eventually losing on points to the big punching Rocky, he was still able to surprise his opponent by taking Rocky the full distance of ten rounds for the very first time.

On 22 June 1949, following the retirement of Joe Louis, Ezzard Charles won the vacant NBA version of the world heavyweight title in Chicago, USA, by outpointing opponent Jersey Joe Walcott over fifteen rounds. On this occasion a new record had been created, since Walcott had become the first man in the division to challenge for the crown on three successive occasions. The first attempt by Walcott took place in New York on 5 December 1947, when defending champion Joe Louis outpointed him over fifteen rounds. The second challenge once again took place in New York on 25 June 1948, when Joe Louis knocked him out in eleven rounds.

In Philadelphia, USA, on 8 February 1950, future world heavyweight champion Jersey Joe Walcott knocked out future world light-heavyweight title-holder Harold Johnson in three rounds.

Now turn the clock back to 22 June 1936: once again the location is Philadelphia and the result is a victory for Jersey Joe by way of a three-round stoppage – the opponent on this occasion being *Phil* Johnson, the father of Harold Johnson.

On 6 June 1950 the British and Empire heavyweight champion Bruce Woodcock met American Lee Savold in a contest which was given recognition by the British Boxing Board of Control and the EBU as being fought for the vacant world heavyweight title. This event came about following the retirement of Joe Louis.

However, in the USA on 22 June 1949, Ezzard Charles had won the NBA version of the championship with a fifteen-round points decision over Jersey Joe

Walcott. Savold won when Woodcock retired in round four of a contest that took place at White City in London. In truth, Savold's claim to the title was not taken too seriously, and on 15 June 1951 Lee was knocked out in six rounds by Joe Louis, who was then on the comeback trail. As a result, any claim Savold had on the championship disappeared completely with that defeat.

Now out of retirement, Joe Louis failed to regain the world heavyweight championship on 27 September 1950 when Ezzard Charles made the fourth defence of the championship, outpointing Louis over fifteen rounds in New York.

However, in this contest Louis created a new record, having made twenty-five defences and overall having taken part in more world heavyweight title bouts (twenty-seven in total) than any other fighter in the history of the sport to date.

When Joe Louis said goodbye to boxing he left with yet another magnificent record, having won twenty-three of his twenty-seven world titles bouts inside the scheduled distance (this figure includes a disqualification victory). No other heavyweight title-holder at that time had ever won that many bouts in a world heavyweight contest before the final bell had rung.

Jack Gardner won the British and Empire heavyweight titles on 14 November 1950 at Earls Court in London, when defending champion Bruce Woodcock retired in round eleven. In doing so, Gardner became the first former ABA heavyweight champion to win these titles (Gardner had won the ABA heavyweight crown in 1948).

CHAMPIONSHIP FIGHTS FOR JOE LOUIS

OPPONENT	RESULT	DATE
James J. Braddock	knockout in round eight (won title)	22 Jun 1937
Tommy Farr	fifteen-round points decision	30 Aug 1937
Nathan Mann	knockout in round three	23 Feb 1938
Harry Thomas	knockout in round five	1 April 1938
Max Schmeling	retired in the first round	22 Jun 1938
John Henry Lewis	stoppage in the first round	25 Jan 1939
Jack Roper	knockout in the first round	17 Apr 1939
Tony Galento	stoppage in round four	28 Jun 1939
Bob Pastor	knockout in round eleven	20 Sep 1939
Arturo Godoy	fifteen-round points decision	9 Feb 1940
Johnny Paychek	stoppage in round two	29 Mar 1940
Arturo Godoy	stoppage in round eight	20 Jun 1940
Al McCoy	opponent retired in round six	16 Dec 1940
Red Burman	knockout in round five	31 Jan 1941
Gus Dorazio	knockout in round two	17 Feb 1941
Abe Simon	stoppage in round thirteen	21 Mar 1941
Tony Musto	stoppage in round nine	8 Apr 1941
Buddy Baer	opponent disqualified in round seven	23 May 1941
Billy Conn	knockout in round thirteen	18 Jun 1941
Lou Nova	stoppage in round six	29 Sep 1941
Buddy Baer	knockout in first round	9 Jan 1942
Abe Simon	knockout in round six	27 Mar 1942
Billy Conn	knockout in round eight	19 Jun 1946
Tami Mauriello	knockout in first round	18 Sep 1946
Jersey Joe Walcot	fifteen-round points decision	5 Dec 1947
Jersey Joe Walcott	knockout in round eleven	25 Jun 1948
Ezzard Charles	lost on a fifteen-round points decision (failed to regain title)	27 Sep 1950

American Arthur Donovan created a record during the course of his career by refereeing more world heavyweight title fights than any other official (the total being fourteen in all). Donovan was the third man in the following bouts:

★ ARTHUR DONOVAN'S REFEREEING CAREER ★

Primo Carnera v. Jack Sharkey	29 Jun 1933
Max Baer v. Primo Carnera	14 Jun 1934
Joe Louis v. Tommy Farr	30 Aug 1937
Joe Louis v. Nathan Mann	23 Feb 1938
Joe Louis v. Max Schmeling	22 Jun 1938
Joe Louis v. John Henry Lewis	25 Jan 1939
Joe Louis v. Tony Galento	28 Jun 1939
Joe Louis v. Arturo Godoy	9 Feb 1940
Joe Louis v. Johnny Paychek	29 Mar 1940
Joe Louis v. Red Burman	31 Jan 1941
Joe Louis v. Tony Musto	8 Apr 1941
Joe Louis v. Buddy Baer	23 May 1941
Joe Louis v. Lou Nova	29 Sep 1941
Joe Louis v. Tami Mauriello	18 Sep 1946

When Jersey Joe Walcott knocked out defending champion Ezzard Charles in seven rounds to win the NY/NBA world crown on 18 July 1951 in Pittsburgh, Pennsylvania, he became, at the age of thirty-seven years, five months and eighteen days, the oldest man at that time to win a version of the heavyweight championship.

It took Jersey Joe Walcott an amazing five attempts to win the heavyweight championship of the world. No fighter at that time had challenged as often as Walcott had for the crown.

Walcott's first attempt took place in New York on 5 December 1947 when he was outpointed over fifteen rounds by defending champion Joe Louis. On 25 June 1948, in a return contest (which also took place in New York) Walcott was knocked out in eleven rounds.

On 22 June 1949, following the retirement of Louis, Jersey Joe contested the vacant NBA crown in Chicago against Ezzard Charles. But once again he failed to lift the title when outpointed over fifteen rounds.

Walcott's fourth attempt took place in Detroit, USA, on 7 March 1951 against the man who had previously defeated him for the vacant title, Ezzard Charles, and yet again Walcott was outpointed over fifteen rounds.

Then, on 18 July 1951, in Pittsburgh, Pennsylvania, the amazing Jersey Joe provided the boxing world with a shock when, in his *fifth* attempt at the championship, he knocked out Ezzard Charles in round seven to win the title.

On 26 October 1951 the curtain came down on the professional boxing career of former heavyweight champion Joe Louis when he faced Rocky Marciano in New York. Stopped by Marciano in round eight, this proved to be Joe's last contest and, while it was somewhat sad to see him bow out of the sport with a defeat, he could take some comfort from the fact that Marciano, like Joe, went on to be considered one of the greats of the division.

On 5 June 1952 Jersey Joe Walcott made the first defence of his world title against former champion Ezzard Charles in Philadelphia, retaining his crown with a fifteen-round points decision. The bout provided an historical chapter to boxing, since official Zack Clayton became the first black referee to handle a world heavyweight title fight.

In the 1952 Olympic Games in Helsinki, Finland, American Ed Sanders won the gold medal when Ingemar Johansson of Sweden was disqualified in round two for not giving his best. Such was the furore at the time that Johansson was not given his silver medal until thirty years later when the International Olympic Committee decided to forgive him for his performance at the time.

During his reign Rocky Marciano defended his world heavyweight title on six occasions with only one challenger going the full distance of fifteen rounds with the hard-punching champion: the former world champion Ezzard Charles, who was outpointed by Marciano in New York on 17 June 1954.

When Ezzard Charles was knocked out in round eight on 17 September 1954 by defending world heavyweight champion Rocky Marciano in New York, he became the first former champion to challenge three times for his old title.

Charles' first attempt had taken place on 5 June 1952 in Philadelphia, Pennsylvania, against the man who eventually beat him – Jersey Joe Walcott – on a fifteen-round points decision.

Charles' second bite at the apple had taken place on 17 June 1954. Once again a fifteen-round points decision against champion Rocky Marciano in New York went against him.

On 16 May 1955 Don Cockell stepped into the ring in San Francisco to become the first British boxer to challenge for the undisputed world heavyweight championship since Tommy Farr, who had pushed the then defending champion Joe Louis all the way in a brave bid on 30 August 1937.

While Cockell put up a gallant effort to win the championship, reigning title-holder Rocky Marciano retained the crown when the contest was stopped in round nine.

Rocky Marciano, who won the world heavyweight title by knocking out defending champion Jersey Joe Walcott in thirteen rounds on 23 September 1952, became the first heavyweight to retire from boxing with a one hundred per cent record, being undefeated in forty-nine professional bouts.

Rocky's last contest took place on 21 September 1955 in New York against challenger Archie Moore, who was counted out in round nine. At the time Moore was the reigning world light-heavyweight champion.

At Earls Court in London on 1 May 1956, Henry Cooper stopped Brian London in the first round. In so doing Henry took revenge and regained his family honour, since Brian had stopped Jim Cooper in four rounds in a contest which had taken place in Streatham, London, on 17 January 1956.

And who exactly was Jim Cooper? Only Henry's twin brother!

In Bologna, Italy, on 30 September 1956, Ingemar Johansson won the European heavyweight crown when he knocked out defending title-holder Franco Cavicchi of Italy in round thirteen. By doing so, Johansson became the first Swedish boxer to win this championship since Olle Tandberg, who won and lost the title in 1943.

Following the retirement of Rocky Marciano, American Floyd Patterson won the vacant world heavyweight championship in Chicago, USA, on 30 November 1956, knocking out former world light-heavyweight king Archie Moore in five rounds. In doing so Patterson added a new chapter to the history of boxing by becoming the youngest man at that time to hold the heavyweight crown. Born on 4 January 1935, Floyd was aged twenty-one years, ten months and twenty-six days at the time of his victory over Moore.

When Floyd Patterson won the world heavyweight championship he became the first ever Olympic gold medal winner to capture this title. Patterson won gold at middleweight at the 1952 Olympic Games in Helsinki, Finland.

On 4 May 1957 Noburu Kataoka punched his way into the history books when he became the first holder of the Japanese heavyweight championship, outpointing opponent Yutaka Nakagoshi over ten rounds for the vacant crown. The contest took place in Tokyo, Japan.

At the Melbourne Olympic Games of 1956, American Pete Rademacher won the gold medal in the heavyweight division. Then, in Seattle, USA, on 22 August 1957, Rademacher had his first professional contest and it is amazing to relate that it was for the world heavyweight title. There is nothing like being thrown in at the deep end! No fighter in the history of the sport had ever challenged for the title in his very first outing in the paid ranks.

However, there was no fairy-tale ending in Seattle, since Rademacher failed in his brave attempt to win the crown when defending champion Floyd Patterson knocked him out in round six to retain the title.

The Patterson–Rademacher contest in 1957 was the first occasion on which two former Olympic gold medal winners had fought each other for the world heavyweight championship.

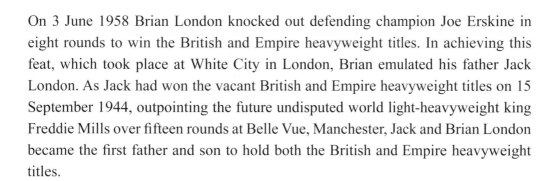

On 3 June 1958 Brian London knocked out defending champion Joe Erskine in eight rounds to win the British and Empire heavyweight titles. In achieving this feat, which took place at White City in London, Brian emulated his father Jack London. As Jack had won the vacant British and Empire heavyweight titles on 15 September 1944, outpointing the future undisputed world light-heavyweight king Freddie Mills over fifteen rounds at Belle Vue, Manchester, Jack and Brian London became the first father and son to hold both the British and Empire heavyweight titles.

Ingemar Johansson sent out a warning to the heavyweight boxing division that he was for real when, on 14 September 1958, he knocked out the highly ranked American contender Eddie Machen in round one of a contest that took place in Gothenburg, Sweden.

Henry Cooper won the British and Empire heavyweight titles on 12 January 1959 when he outpointed holder Brian London over fifteen rounds at Earls Court, London. In many ways this victory was a tribute to this boxer's fighting heart, since Cooper's chance of being any kind of title-holder looked very slim when he had a bad run of four successive defeats.

On 7 September 1956 he lost to Peter Bates in Manchester when he retired in round five. On 19 February 1957 at Earls Court in London, he was knocked out by holder Joe Bygraves of Jamaica in round nine when challenging for the Empire crown. He once again came up short when, on 19 May 1957, he challenged Sweden's Ingemar Johansson for the European title in Stockholm, Sweden – Cooper was counted out in round five. Nor did his luck change for the better on 17 September 1957 when challenging Joe Erskine for the British heavyweight crown at Harringay in London, this time being at the wrong end of a fifteen-round points decision.

By now, a lesser man would have started to think that he had no chance of ever winning a professional title and perhaps another line of work might be a wise option. However, Henry never gave up; clearly the word 'quit' was not in his vocabulary. He regrouped and went back into action, putting a string of victories together and fighting his way back to a championship challenge.

During his career, Welshman Joe Erskine had a number of victories over quality fighters, but perhaps his best on the international front was his ten-round points win at Wembley on 24 February 1959 against American Willie Pastrano. For, on 1 June 1963, Pastrano captured the world light-heavyweight crown in Las Vegas, USA, outpointing defending champion Harold Johnson over fifteen rounds.

On 26 June 1959 Sweden's Ingemar Johansson caused an upset when he stopped defending champion Floyd Patterson in three rounds in New York to become king of the heavyweight division. In doing so, Johansson became the first European boxer to hold the championship since Italy's Primo Carnera.

When Ingemar Johansson won the world heavyweight championship he became the first non-American to do so with an undefeated professional record, going into the contest against Floyd Patterson with a tally of twenty-one winning bouts and no defeats.

Cuban fighter Nino Valdes was bad news for British heavyweights: a one-man wrecking-machine – a destroyer. His motto seemed to be 'stand 'em up and I'll knock 'em down'.

At Wembley on 1 December 1959, Valdes defeated former British and Empire heavyweight champion Brian London, who was stopped in round seven. Nino had also defeated home fighters in impressive style on his three previous visits to the British Isles. His run of victories began on 13 September 1955 at White City in London when the Cuban stopped Don Cockell in round three. Cockell was the reigning British and Empire heavyweight champion and former British, European and Empire light-heavyweight king. In his last contest on 16 May 1955 he had bravely challenged Rocky Marciano for the world heavyweight crown, but was stopped in round nine.

Dick Richardson was the next fighter to share the ring with Valdes, at Harringay in north London on 4 December 1956. However, the future European heavyweight champion was another who failed to last the distance, let alone win, when he was stopped in round eight.

The third visit for Valdes took place on 19 February 1957 at Earls Court, west London. In the opposite corner was British heavyweight champion Joe Erskine, who did not hear the bell to start round two – he was disposed of by way of a stoppage in the first round.

On 27 March 1960 Welshman Dick Richardson travelled to Dortmund, West Germany, to contest the vacant European heavyweight title against German Hans Kalbfell. Despite fighting in the Lion's Den, Richardson pulled off a magnificent victory by stopping his opponent in round thirteen. Richardson thus became the first British boxer to win the European heavyweight championship abroad.

Derek Rowe

In 1960 Floyd Patterson became the first man to regain the world heavyweight title when he knocked out defending champion Ingemar Johansson in the fifth round

Floyd Patterson produced a knockout piece of boxing history on 20 June 1960 when, in New York, he became the first fighter to regain the world heavyweight championship, knocking out Ingemar Johansson in round five.

On 29 August 1960 Welshman Dick Richardson made the first defence of his European title against former British and Empire heavyweight king Brian London at Coney Beach Arena, Porthcawl. This marked the first occasion for a European heavyweight contest to be staged in South Wales.

That evening the Welsh Dragon roared, for Richardson retained the championship when London retired in round eight. Sadly, the occasion was marred by an after-fight brawl in the ring. Both boxers and their respective cornermen were involved and police had to enter the ring to restore order!

CHAPTER FOUR

THE ERA OF MUHAMMAD ALI

Cassius Clay (later to become Muhammad Ali), the Rome 1960 light-heavyweight Olympic gold medallist, made his professional debut in Louisville, Kentucky, USA, on 29 October 1960, outpointing opponent Tunney Hunsaker over six rounds.

On 18 February 1961, Dick Richardson returned to West Germany to make the second defence of his European title, outpointing Hans Kalbfell over fifteen rounds in Dortmund. In retaining the crown, Richardson had the distinction of becoming the first British heavyweight to make a successful defence of the European heavyweight title abroad.

When Floyd Patterson defended his world heavyweight title against challenger Ingemar Johansson on 13 March 1961, it became the first time in the history of the division for the same two men to meet on three successive occasions for the championship.

On this third occasion, Patterson retained his crown in Miami, Florida, with a six-round knockout.

In boxing, often new rules are introduced from time to time to improve the safety of the boxers taking part in a contest.

The third encounter between Floyd Patterson and Ingemar Johansson saw the mandatory eight count introduced for the first time in a world heavyweight title contest. On being floored, a boxer had to take a count of eight from the referee before he would be allowed to continue.

The third Patterson–Johansson contest in 1961 also saw the twenty-second count introduced for the first time in a world heavyweight title bout. Should either boxer be knocked out of the ring during the contest, the referee would give him twenty seconds to return to the ring before being counted out.

It was an astonishingly successful night for British amateur boxing on 2 November 1961, when Great Britain defeated America ten bouts to nil. Alan Rudkin (flyweight), Peter Bennyworth (bantamweight), Frankie Taylor (featherweight), Dick McTaggart (lightweight), Brian Brazier (light-welterweight), Jim Lloyd (welterweight), Derek Richards (light-middleweight), John Fisher (middleweight), and Dennis Pollard (light-heavyweight) all had impressive wins over their opponents.

However, without doubt the night belonged to heavyweight Billy Walker who had the tough task of crossing gloves with Cornelius Perry from Philadelphia, USA. Hopes of a British victory were remote since the man from Philly looked unstoppable. Yet, on the night Billy was a revelation, knocking out his opponent in the first round. This was a sensational victory for Billy, who became a household name after this fine performance.

Derek Rowe

Billy Walker did not win a title in the professional ranks but this exciting fighter was the undisputed box-office champion, with fans flocking to see his fights

Jersey Joe Walcott became just the second former world heavyweight champion to referee a world heavyweight title fight on 4 December 1961. The contest in question was the defence of the crown by Floyd Patterson, who duly stopped challenger Tom McNeeley of America in four rounds.

The encounter took place in Toronto – something of a milestone in itself since it was the first time that a world heavyweight title contest had taken place in Canada.

In 1961 Floyd Patterson became the first American world champion since Jack Johnson to defend the world heavyweight title outside the USA

Les Clark

When Floyd Patterson defeated challenger Tom McNeeley in defence of his world crown he became the first American world heavyweight champion to defend his crown outside the USA since Jack Johnson, who had lost his title to fellow American Jess Willard in Havana, Cuba, in April 1915 by a knockout in round twenty-six.

On 5 December 1961 American Zora Folley knocked out the then reigning British and Empire heavyweight champion Henry Cooper in two rounds at Wembley, London. This was sweet revenge for Folley, as in a previous encounter that had taken place on 14 October 1958, Cooper had outpointed the American over ten rounds (also at Wembley), giving Cooper at that particular time his best victory over a highly ranked opponent.

The first man to floor Cassius Clay in the professional ranks was Sonny Banks. This event took place in New York. Clay was having his eleventh paid contest on 10 February 1962 when Banks introduced him to the canvas in round one. However, Clay made him pay for this indignity and duly fought back to stop his opponent in round four.

West Germany proved to be a happy hunting ground for Britain's Dick Richardson, who both won and then defended his European heavyweight title in this country. Now his fourth European contest (third in West Germany) saw him once again in action in Dortmund. Would he score a hat-trick? The answer was a resounding yes when, on 24 February 1962, Richardson retained his crown by knocking out challenger Karl Mildenberger in the first round.

Mildenberger later went on to win the European heavyweight title in 1964 and then become a ranked contender who challenged Cassius Clay (now Muhammad Ali) for the world crown in 1966.

On 2 April 1962 Henry Cooper retained his British and Empire heavyweight titles when he stopped former British and Empire champion Joe Erskine in round nine in a contest in Nottingham. This was their fifth meeting in a professional ring.

On 15 November 1955 the two crossed gloves for the first time in the paid ranks at Harringay, London, in a British heavyweight title eliminator. On this occasion Erskine won a ten-round points decision.

In their second meeting, also at Harringay, on 17 September 1957, Erskine (who was then the British heavyweight champion) outpointed Cooper over fifteen rounds to retain the title.

In their next encounter, on 17 November 1959, the tables were turned: Cooper was now the British and Empire heavyweight champion. Henry had taken the British and Empire heavyweight titles from Brian London on 12 January 1959 by way of a fifteen-round points decision – London having won the titles knocking out Erskine in eight rounds on 3 June 1958. Cooper remained the champion at Earls Court, stopping Erskine in round twelve.

The pair went to battle once again on 21 March 1961 at Wembley, and once again Henry fought his way to another victory and retained his British and Empire heavyweight crown when Joe retired in round five.

The contest in 1962 proved to be the last time the boxers would exchange blows in what had been an excellent series of bouts, with the score standing at Cooper three, Erskine two.

In Gothenburg, Sweden, on 17 June 1962, former world heavyweight champion Ingemar Johansson regained his European title when he knocked out holder Dick Richardson in the eighth round. At that time, Richardson had taken part in more European heavyweight title contests than any other British boxer – the number being five in total.

On 25 September 1962 Floyd Patterson became the first defending world heavyweight champion to lose his title by a knockout in round one. The man who took the crown in Chicago was the then-fearsome Sonny Liston.

On 26 March 1963 Henry Cooper retained his British and Empire heavyweight titles at Wembley, London, by knocking out former European champion Dick Richardson in round five.

Clearly five was an unlucky number for Richardson where Cooper was concerned, for in a previous non-title encounter in Porthcawl, South Wales, on 3 September 1958, Henry stopped him once again in the fifth round.

On 21 April 1963 former British and Empire heavyweight champion Brian London fought former world heavyweight title-holder Ingemar Johansson in Stockholm, Sweden, in a bout scheduled for twelve rounds. Johansson won on points in what was his last professional appearance inside a boxing ring.

Cassius Clay's first professional contest abroad took place in England on 18 June 1963. The opponent for Clay was British and Empire heavyweight champion Henry Cooper. Clay won his bout when the referee duly stopped the bout in round

Henry Cooper went on to become the only man in the history of British boxing to win three Lonsdale belts outright

five, but not before Cassius found himself on the canvas in round four, courtesy of Henry's famed left hook, registering just the second knockdown in the American's career to date.

Who said lightning doesn't strike twice? Floyd Patterson attempted to regain his world heavyweight title in Las Vegas on 22 July 1963, but failed when the thunderous fists of Sonny Liston ended his attempt once again in the very first round. This meant that Floyd was the first man in the division to be knocked out twice in the first round when contesting a world heavyweight championship.

Henry Cooper became the first man in the division to win two Lonsdale belts outright on 24 February 1964 at Belle Vue, Manchester.

Cooper outpointed Brian London over fifteen rounds to retain his British heavyweight title and Empire crown. In doing so, Cooper picked up the vacant European championship which was also at stake. To win two Lonsdale belts outright a boxer had to gain six British title victories – no mean feat.

Cassius Clay won the world heavyweight championship in Miami, Florida, on 25 February 1964 when holder Sonny Liston retired on his stool in his corner at the end of round six. Thus, Liston became just the second defending world champion in the division to retire in the corner. The first title-holder to do so had been Jess Willard in 1919 when losing the crown to Jack Dempsey.

On 12 May 1964 at Wembley, London, British heavyweight Billy Walker knocked out American Bill Nielsen in two rounds, giving Walker revenge for an eight-round cut eye defeat he suffered in their previous match, which had taken place in London on 10 March 1964.

The contest not only gave Billy a good victory on the night, but also saw two new significant changes to British boxing: for the first time, blood relations were allowed in the corner of the fighter. This duly meant that Billy's brother George, who was his manager, could now be with him in the respective corner.

Walker wore a pair of white shorts on the night – the first time white shorts could be worn in the ring by a fighter.

During his professional career, American Chip Johnson boxed five times in Britain. The first bout was against Johnny Prescott in Birmingham on 29 September 1964. The result was a draw over ten rounds.

The second contest took place in Manchester against Jim Cooper (Henry's twin brother) on 9 November 1964. The visitor had his hand raised in victory when Cooper was stopped in round three.

Next up was former British and Empire heavyweight champion Brian London, who faced Johnson in Wolverhampton, West Midlands, on 15 December 1964. London emerged victorious when the referee stopped the bout in the fourth round.

Reigning British and Empire heavyweight champion Henry Cooper made short work of the American in Wolverhampton on 20 April 1965, winning by a knockout in the first round. A return with Johnny Prescott on 19 October 1965 at Wembley in London once again saw Johnson defeated when the referee stopped the bout in round five.

When Muhammad Ali signed to meet Sonny Liston in a return contest for the world heavyweight title, the WBA stripped their version of the championship from him and thus nominated Ernie Terrell to meet Eddie Machen for the vacant crown. On 5 March 1965 in Chicago, USA, Terrell outpointed Machen over fifteen rounds to become the WBA's new title-holder. In doing so, Terrell, at the listed height of

Les Clark

Ernie Terrell (here pictured in later years) won the vacant WBA world heavyweight crown on 5 March 1965 when he outpointed Eddie Machen over fifteen rounds

6 ft 6 inches, became the second tallest man at that time to hold a version of the world heavyweight championship.

Cassius Clay had his first contest under his new name of Muhammad Ali on 25 May 1965 when making the first defence of the world crown in Lewiston, Maine, USA, against the man he took the title from – Sonny Liston. The crown remained in the hands of Ali, who retained the championship by a knockout in round one. The name may have been different but the boxer's outstanding skills were very much the same.

If the words of the song 'Where have all the flowers gone?' by Pete Seeger had been changed to 'Where have all the spectators gone?', it would have been an appropriate theme for the second contest between Muhammad Ali and Sonny Liston, since the fight created a record of having the lowest attendance of any world heavyweight title fight in the history of the sport at that time, with just a reported 2,434 fans turning up to watch the contest.

Angelo Dundee checks the bandages on the hands of Muhammad Ali during a sparring session to ensure that the boxer's hands are properly protected

The first challenger to take champion Muhammad Ali the full distance of fifteen rounds in a world heavyweight title fight was Canada's George Chuvalo. The bout took place on 29 March 1966 in Toronto. Chuvalo, a very tough and brave fighter, gave his all in a rugged bout, but the boxing skills of Ali proved too much for him.

On 21 May 1966 Muhammad Ali retained his WBC world heavyweight championship at Highbury in London, stopping challenger Henry Cooper, the British and Empire heavyweight king, in round six. The third man in this contest was George Smith, who had the honour of being the first Scottish referee to officiate in a world heavyweight championship bout.

67

At Earls Court on 6 August 1966, Brian London challenged Muhammad Ali for the WBC world heavyweight crown, but failed in his attempt to win the title when knocked out in round three. On that occasion Brian became the first modern-day British fighter to challenge twice for the major championship. London's first attempt took place in Indianapolis, USA, on 1 May 1959, against the then defending title-holder Floyd Patterson, who retained the championship by a knockout in the eleventh round.

On 20 September 1966 former two-time world heavyweight champion Floyd Patterson made his first professional visit to Britain to meet Henry Cooper. Both men had lost in their last contests, challenging Muhammad Ali for the WBC world heavyweight crown (Cooper was stopped in round six at Highbury, London, on 21 May 1966 and Patterson in round twelve on 22 November 1965 in Las Vegas, USA). This was an important bout, since a win here was vital for the victor to stay in contention for another possible world title chance sometime in the future. In round four Floyd's hand was raised in victory at Wembley after he knocked out Cooper, much to the disappointment of British fans.

Karl Mildenberger put in a most valiant effort to win the world heavyweight crown on 10 September 1966 in Frankfurt against holder Muhammad Ali in the first ever title fight at the weight to be staged in Germany. However, Mildenberger's southpaw skills were not enough to topple the champion, who duly stopped him in round twelve. Mildenberger was therefore the first German to contest a world heavyweight title since Max Schmeling, who failed to regain the crown on 22 June 1938 from Joe Louis when Schmeling retired in the opening round.

While Karl Mildenberger may have failed to win the title from Muhammad Ali, he could at least take a degree of satisfaction by knowing that he had made a contribution to boxing history by becoming the first man with the southpaw stance to challenge for the world heavyweight championship.

The boxing world once again had an undisputed world heavyweight champion when Muhammad Ali, the WBC holder of the title, met Ernie Terrell, the WBA king, in Houston, Texas, on 6 February 1967. After fifteen rounds Ali was declared the winner on points and thus confirmed, if there was ever any doubt in the eyes of the world, as the best fighter at that weight at that particular time.

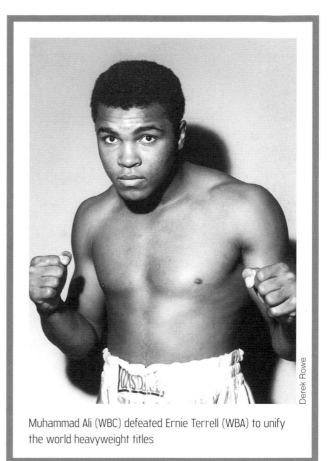

Muhammad Ali (WBC) defeated Ernie Terrell (WBA) to unify the world heavyweight titles

Derek Rowe

In Rome in 1967, Peter Boddington almost became the first English heavyweight to win a gold medal at the Amateur European championships when in the final he lost a three-round points decision to Italy's Mario Baruzzi, and therefore took home a very much deserved silver.

Les Clark

In defence of his British and Commonwealth heavyweight titles, in 1967 Henry Cooper (left) defeated Billy Walker (right), stopping him in round six. The two men met again in 2007 – this time at a book-signing.

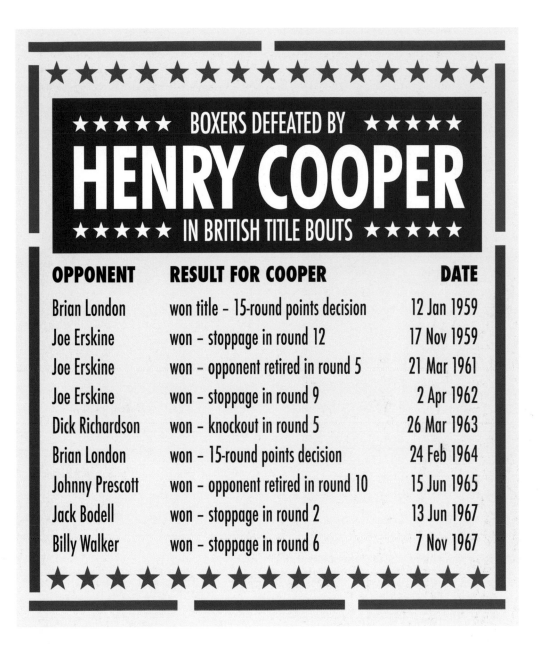

BOXERS DEFEATED BY

HENRY COOPER

IN BRITISH TITLE BOUTS

OPPONENT	RESULT FOR COOPER	DATE
Brian London	won title – 15-round points decision	12 Jan 1959
Joe Erskine	won – stoppage in round 12	17 Nov 1959
Joe Erskine	won – opponent retired in round 5	21 Mar 1961
Joe Erskine	won – stoppage in round 9	2 Apr 1962
Dick Richardson	won – knockout in round 5	26 Mar 1963
Brian London	won – 15-round points decision	24 Feb 1964
Johnny Prescott	won – opponent retired in round 10	15 Jun 1965
Jack Bodell	won – stoppage in round 2	13 Jun 1967
Billy Walker	won – stoppage in round 6	7 Nov 1967

On 7 November 1967 Henry Cooper retained his British and Empire heavyweight titles at Wembley, London, stopping challenger Billy Walker in round six. Thus, Cooper became the first man in the history of the sport to win three Lonsdale belts outright. At that time, a fighter had to win three British title fights to keep the belt

Les Clark

Fans' favourite Billy Walker had his last contest on 25 March 1968 when he was stopped by Jack Bodell in round eight

Joe Bugner had a bad start to his professional career on 20 December 1967, being knocked out by opponent Paul Brown in three rounds at Mayfair in London. However, they say it's not how you start, but how you finish. Joe was later to go on and become a British, European and Commonwealth heavyweight champion, and world title challenger.

Joe Frazier won the vacant New York State version of the world heavyweight title on 4 March 1968 by stopping Buster Mathis in round eleven. Frazier thus became the first Olympic heavyweight gold medal winner (Tokyo, 1964) to achieve the double by also winning a version of the world heavyweight championship in the professional ranks. (Muhammad Ali had been stripped of the title for refusing to join the US army.)

On 25 March 1968, Billy Walker was stopped in the eighth round by Jack Bodell after an exciting fight at Wembley, London. For Billy (nicknamed 'the Blond Bomber') this proved to be his final professional contest. Walker left the sport with a professional record of thirty-one bouts, winning twenty-one, with two draws and eight defeats.

During his period in the pay-ranks, Walker failed to win a championship. Billy was stopped in round eight when challenging Karl Mildenberger for the European title at Wembley on 21 March 1967. He once again came up empty when going up against Henry Cooper at Wembley on 7 November 1967 for the British and Empire heavyweight titles. On this occasion, Walker was stopped in the sixth round.

However, no one can dispute that he was the champion of the box-office, since there were few, if any, empty seats when Walker fought – he was a promoter's dream. Billy always gave his very all, win or lose. As a result, Walker was a big favourite with the fans and in his own way gave the British heavyweight scene a boost during his time in the ring.

Jimmy Ellis won the vacant WBA world heavyweight championship when he outpointed opponent Jerry Quarry over fifteen rounds in Oakland, USA, on 27 April 1968. Now the division had *two* world title-holders at the weight, Joe Frazier being the rival champion.

On 24 June 1968 Manuel Ramos challenged Joe Frazier for the New York State version of the world heavyweight title, but failed to take the crown when he retired in round two. Frazier was just too strong for him in every department.

Ramos may have had a most painful encounter against Frazier, but he put his name in the record books by being the first Mexican to challenge for a world heavyweight title.

Jimmy Ellis retained the WBA version of the world heavyweight championship on 14 September 1968, outpointing challenger and former two-time world heavyweight king Floyd Patterson over fifteen rounds. The contest, which took place in Stockholm, was the first world heavyweight title bout to be staged in Sweden.

Henry Cooper became the first British boxer to regain the European heavyweight title. Cooper accomplished this feat on 18 September 1968 when he defeated defending champion Karl Mildenberger of Germany at Wembley, London, by way of a disqualification in round eight.

It seemed that Italy's Piero Tomasoni was not fated to win the European heavy-weight title, even when given three bites at the apple. On 14 May 1965, Piero challenged champion Karl Mildenberger in Frankfurt, West Germany, losing a fifteen-round points decision.

Then, on 1 February 1967, Tomasoni was given a second shot at the championship against the still reigning title-holder Karl Mildenberger. Once again the contest took place in Frankfurt, with the outcome being the same: a fifteen-round points' defeat for the Italian.

The third challenge took place on Piero's home turf in Rome on 13 March 1969 against Britain's Henry Cooper, who was making his first defence of the title he had taken from Mildenberger. The question was, would it be third time lucky for Piero? The answer was a resounding 'No!' when Cooper's famed left hook found its target in round five. Cooper retained the championship by a knockout.

Former world heavyweight champion Rocky Marciano tragically died on 31 August 1969 when a small plane in which he was a passenger crashed. Rocky was just forty-five years, eleven months and thirty days old at the time of his death (having been born on 1 September 1923).

During his career Rocky fought men of the calibre of Joe Louis, Jersey Joe Walcott (twice), Ezzard Charles (twice), Archie Moore, Don Cockell, and Roland LaStarza.

Derek Rowe

During a visit to London Rocky Marciano (centre) was honoured by a number of British champions past and present, including (from left to right) Don Cockell, Joe Erskine, Henry Cooper, Len Harvey, Jack Petersen, Johnny Williams, and Tommy Farr

By outpointing opponent Carl Gizzi in Nottingham over fifteen rounds on 13 October 1969, Jack Bodell won the vacant British heavyweight title, which had been relinquished by Henry Cooper. Bodell thus put his name in the boxing history books by being the first fighter with the southpaw stance to hold the crown.

In Las Vegas, USA, on 6 December 1969, Leotis Martin knocked out former world heavyweight champion Sonny Liston in round nine to become the first holder of the NABF heavyweight crown.

CHAPTER FIVE

THE GOLDEN AGE OF HEAVYWEIGHT BOXING

When Diana Ross left the top Motown band The Supremes in 1970, she was replaced by vocalist Jean Terrell.
   Jean Terrell had a strong connection with boxing: she was sister of former WBA world heavyweight champion, Ernie Terrell.

Joe Frazier, who held the New York State version of the world heavyweight crown, became the undisputed world heavyweight champion on 16 February 1970 when he met Jimmy Ellis, the rival WBA title-holder, in New York. Frazier won when Ellis retired in round four.

When he met defending title-holder Peter Weiland of West Germany in Madrid, Spain, on 3 April 1970, Jose Urtain became the first Spanish European heavyweight champion since Paulino Uzcudun, who had both won and lost the title in 1933. Urtain's hand was raised in victory when Weiland was counted out in round seven.

Joe Frazier became the undisputed world heavyweight champion in 1970 when he defeated Jimmy Ellis

Les Clark

Derek Rowe

Joe Bugner (pictured) was Brian London's last professional opponent

Former British and Empire heavyweight champion Brian London had his last professional contest on 12 May 1970 at Wembley, being stopped in round five by Joe Bugner.

During his professional career London had taken part in fifty-eight contests, winning thirty-seven, losing twenty and drawing only one of his bouts. London shared the ring with boxers like Muhammad Ali, Floyd Patterson, Ingemar Johansson, Willie Pastrano (twice), Henry Cooper (three times), Joe Erskine, Nino Valdes, Eddie Machen, Thad Spencer, Zora Folley, Jerry Quarry (twice), Dick Richardson, Jack Bodell and Billy Walker.

There was a great deal of excited anticipation amongst boxing fans on 26 October 1970. It was the ring return of Muhammad Ali against Jerry Quarry in Atlanta, USA. Ali's last contest (on 22 March 1967) had been title defence against Zora Folley in New York and had resulted in a seven-round knockout victory for Ali. There then followed an enforced exile from the sport due to Ali's refusal to be drafted into the US army. Now Ali was back and looking to regain his world heavyweight crown. Ali successfully took the first step back towards the title by stopping Quarry in three rounds. From now on it was a case of onwards and upwards for Ali.

Henry Cooper became the first British boxer to regain the European heavyweight title twice when, on 10 November 1970, he stopped Spain's defending champion Jose Urtain in round nine, in a contest that took place at Wembley, London. The then much praised Urtain was no match for the skill and punching power of the English challenger.

Muhammad Ali met with his first professional defeat on 8 March 1971 in New York, USA, when attempting to regain his world heavyweight championship from holder Joe Frazier. After fifteen hard-fought rounds Frazier emerged the victor and still champion after being given the points decision.

Going into the contest Ali had been undefeated in thirty-one bouts and Frazier too had yet to meet defeat with a 100 per cent record of twenty-six wins. (At the time of the contest, Frazier was the undisputed champion after defeating rival WBA title-holder Jimmy Ellis in 1970.)

On 8 March 1971 Danny McAlinden made his American debut in New York a winning one when he outpointed Rahman Ali over six rounds. Rahman was the younger brother of Muhammad Ali.

It was clearly an end to an era on 16 March 1971 when Joe Bugner outpointed defending champion Henry Cooper over fifteen rounds at Wembley to capture the British, European and Commonwealth heavyweight titles. Cooper had been the top heavyweight in British boxing for many years and he retired after this defeat.

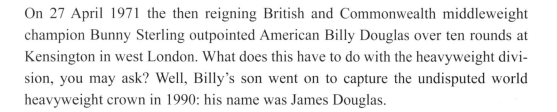

On 27 April 1971 the then reigning British and Commonwealth middleweight champion Bunny Sterling outpointed American Billy Douglas over ten rounds at Kensington in west London. What does this have to do with the heavyweight division, you may ask? Well, Billy's son went on to capture the undisputed world heavyweight crown in 1990: his name was James Douglas.

Muhammad Ali returned to winning ways on 26 July 1971, following his defeat against Joe Frazier, when he fought former WBA world heavyweight title-holder Jimmy Ellis in Houston, Texas. Ali won when he stopped Ellis in round twelve to collect the vacant NABF championship and hence get his career back on track.

Former British champion Jack Bodell provided a shock on 27 September 1971 when he outpointed defending champion Joe Bugner over fifteen rounds to capture the British, European and Commonwealth heavyweight titles at Wembley.

Bodell was a worthy challenger, but it was strongly felt before the contest that Bugner would emerge the victor since he was the man who looked headed for big things on the boxing front. However, Jack had not come to the ring just to make up the numbers and clearly he hadn't read the script! Bodell was ready to rock'n'roll: he took control of the fight in no uncertain manner, racking up the points to be the clear winner.

As Bodell had been the first boxer with the southpaw stance to win the British heavyweight crown, he could now claim to be first southpaw to have *regained* the said championship.

American heavyweight contender Jerry Quarry made his professional British debut on 16 November 1971 when he met reigning British, European and Commonwealth heavyweight champion Jack Bodell at Wembley. This particular bout was scheduled for ten rounds. However, the contest was all over in the first when Quarry scored a knockout victory.

In the past Quarry had fought men like Eddie Machen, Floyd Patterson (twice), Thad Spencer, Jimmy Ellis, Joe Frazier, Muhammad Ali, George Chuvalo, Brian London (twice), and Buster Mathis.

On 27 June 1972 Mike Quarry challenged reigning title-holder Bob Foster for the world light-heavyweight championship in Las Vegas, but failed in his bid when knocked out in round four. Mike was the younger brother of former world heavyweight title challenger Jerry Quarry.

Irish eyes were certainly smiling when Danny McAlinden knocked out holder Jack Bodell in two rounds in Birmingham on 27 June 1972 to win the British and Commonwealth heavyweight titles. McAlinden became the first Irishman to win the British crown since the formation of the British Boxing Board of Control in 1929.

This was Bodell's second reign as British champion. Earlier, on 24 March 1970, he had lost the title to Henry Cooper, having been outpointed over fifteen rounds. Bodell then regained the British championship along with the Commonwealth and European title by outpointing then holder Joe Bugner over fifteen rounds).

Previously, on 17 December 1971, Bodell had lost the European crown to Jose Urtain.

In the Munich Olympic Games of 1972, Teófilo Stevenson of Cuba won the gold medal in the heavyweight division. On this occasion he also became the first boxer

Derek Rowe

Danny McAlinden was the first Irish-born boxer to win the British heavyweight title in June 1972 when he knocked out defending champion Jack Bodell in the second round

On 22 January 1973 George Foreman (here on the left with boxing promoter Jack Solomons) became the first man in the professional ranks to defeat Joe Frazier when winning the world title

at heavyweight to win The Val Barker Trophy. This award, introduced in 1936, was awarded to the most stylish boxer of each respective Olympic competition.

On 22 January 1973 a world heavyweight title fight took place in Jamaica for the very first time. The contest in Kingston did not last long: Joe Frazier lost his world heavyweight championship to fellow America George Foreman in no uncertain manner by a stoppage in round two.

Going into the contest it had been a battle of the undefeated as Foreman had won all thirty-seven of his professional bouts to date and Frazier all twenty-nine of his.

When Joe Frazier and George Foreman fought for the world title, it was something of an historical event. This was the first time two former Olympic heavyweight gold medallists had met in a professional ring to battle against each other for the world heavyweight crown.

Frazier had struck gold at heavyweight in the 1964 games, held in Tokyo, Japan, and Foreman had captured gold in Mexico in 1968.

On 31 March 1973 Ken Norton provided the world of boxing with a shock. In a contest which took place in San Diego, the former Marine outpointed Muhammad Ali over twelve rounds to give the former world heavyweight champion his second defeat in the professional ranks. During the bout, Ali suffered a broken jaw and also lost his NABF heavyweight crown.

The two boxers met on two further occasions. On 10 September 1973 Ali outpointed Norton over twelve rounds in Los Angeles to gain revenge (and thus regain his NABF crown). Then, on 28 September 1976, as the then reigning world heavyweight champion, Ali successfully defended his crown against Norton, outpointing him over fifteen rounds in New York.

Japan had its first ever world heavyweight title contest on 1 September 1973 when George Foreman made the first defence of his championship in Tokyo. However, the fans did not see much action since big punching George was clearly in a hurry, sending the fans home early by knocking out challenger Jose Roman in the first round. Clearly, when Foreman was in the ring the fans had no-chance of missing the last bus home – such was the speed of his victories.

Jose Roman's 1973 challenge to George Foreman did not last long, but he can claim to be the first Puerto Rican to contest the world heavyweight championship.

George Foreman appeared to be a champion with the 'Have Gloves, Will Travel' temperament. His second defence of the world title took place in Caracas, Venezuela, on 26 March 1974 against fellow American Ken Norton. This was the first world heavyweight championship contest to be staged in Venezuela. However, once again the fans did not see a great deal of George for the bout was over in round two, with Foreman retaining the title by way of a stoppage. Without doubt, George was not one for hanging around too long in the ring.

Muhammad Ali really established himself in the history of boxing when, on 30 October 1974 in Kinshasa, he became just the second man to regain the world heavyweight championship by knocking out holder George Foreman in round eight.

Foreman had been used to sending his opponents back to their dressing rooms in double quick time, however Ali was able to withstand his formidable punching power and thus land his own telling blows to terminate the fight in his favour. Going into the contest Foreman had been undefeated in forty professional bouts with Ali's record standing at forty-four wins with just two defeats.

This contest was also notable for being the first heavyweight championship to be staged in Zaire.

During his first reign as world heavyweight champion, George Foreman became the first American holder of this crown not to have one title bout in his own country. All his championship bouts took place outside the USA in Jamaica, Japan, Venezuela, and Zaire.

The luck of the Irish appeared to desert Danny McAlinden on 13 January 1975 in Mayfair, London, when he lost his British heavyweight championship by way of a knockout in round nine to challenger Bunny Johnson. Thus, Johnson put his name in the record books by becoming the first black fighter to win this crown. Bunny also won the Commonwealth title which McAlinden was also defending.

On 24 March 1975 in Cleveland, Ohio, during a challenge for the world heavyweight title, Chuck Wepner was stopped in round fifteen by Muhammad Ali. However, Wepner became the first man to floor Ali (round nine) for a count while he was the defending champion.

It was speculated that watching the Ali–Wepner encounter gave actor Sylvester Stallone the inspiration to write *Rocky*. The film went on to become a worldwide, box-office hit, with several sequels.

In the first world heavyweight championship to be staged in Malaysia, Joe Bugner failed to win the title when he lost a fifteen-round points decision to holder Muhammad Ali in Kuala Lumpur on 1 July 1975. However, Bugner did become the first British challenger to last the distance in a heavyweight title fight since Tommy Farr, who had battled all the way against the then champion Joe Louis in 1937.

Richard Dunn became just the second fighter with the southpaw stance to win the British heavyweight title when he outpointed defending champion Bunny Johnson at Wembley over fifteen rounds on 30 September 1975.

Muhammad Ali (seated right) and Joe Bugner (seated left) in a press conference after their Valentine's Day contest in 1973. The pair met again in Kuala Lumpur in July 1975, when Ali retained his world heavyweight title.

During this encounter, Dunn also captured the Commonwealth championship, which Johnson was also defending.

A contest which many say was the best ever world heavyweight title fight to be staged at that time in the history of the sport took place on 1 October 1975 in the Philippines. The first ever world championship fight in the division to be held in this country proved to be a magnificent contest. Muhammad Ali was putting his crown on the line against former champion Joe Frazier, and Ali retained his championship when Frazier retired in round fourteen.

In the contest – dubbed 'The Thriller in Manila' – both men displayed courage and dignity far beyond the call of duty in a splendid and breath-taking encounter, which had the watching fans on the very edge of their seats with pure excitement.

Muhammad Ali successfully defended his world title on 20 February 1976 against challenger Jean-Pierre Coopman by a knockout in round five. This was the first world heavyweight title fight to take place in Puerto Rico.

Derek Rowe

Richard Dunn became just the second boxer with the southpaw stance to win the British heavyweight title when he outpointed holder Bunny Johnson over fifteen rounds on 30 September 1975

When Jean-Pierre Coopman challenged Muhammad Ali for the title he became the first boxer from Belgium to contest the world heavyweight championship.

Richard Dunn, the then reigning British, European and Commonwealth heavyweight champion, challenged Muhammad Ali for the world title on 25 May 1976 in Munich, West Germany. The championship remained in the American's hands when the contest was stopped in Ali's favour in round five. In the event, Dunn became the last opponent that Muhammad Ali was to stop inside the scheduled distance.

On 25 June 1976 world heavyweight champion Muhammad Ali met Antonio Inoki in a boxer v. wrestler exhibition bout in Tokyo, Japan. At the end of fifteen indifferent rounds the bout was declared a draw.

On 5 March 1977 American Leon Spinks, the 1976 Olympic light-heavyweight gold medallist, had his second professional contest against opponent Peter Freeman in Liverpool, England, knocking out his British opponent in the first round.

In due course, Spinks was to go on to win the world heavyweight crown and in so doing become only the third man in the professional ranks to defeat Muhammad Ali (Joe Frazier and Ken Norton being the first two boxers to have achieved this feat).

It is not unusual for a British light-heavyweight champion to move up a division to heavyweight and attempt to win the British title at that poundage. However, it is unusual for a former champion at the heavier weight to move *down* a division and try his luck there. Bunny Johnson pulled off a first when he did just that in Wolverhampton, England, on 8 March 1977.

During the match, the former British and Commonwealth heavyweight champion challenged the reigning British light-heavyweight king Tim Wood, quickly despatching him by a knockout in the very first round to win the title.

British boxer Len Harvey lost the British and Empire heavyweight titles to Jack Petersen by a twelve-round retirement on 4 June 1934 at White City, London. After failing to regain these titles from Petersen on 29 January 1936 at Wembley (when he was outpointed over fifteen rounds), Harvey then moved down to light-heavyweight, and on 7 April 1938 he outpointed title-holder Jock McAvoy over fifteen rounds at Harringay for the British crown.

Therefore, some might then argue (with a degree of justification) that Harvey was in fact the first former British heavyweight champion to accomplish this feat. However, it should be taken into consideration that Harvey was a former holder of the British light-heavyweight title first, whereas Bunny Johnson was British heavyweight champion *before* he was a British light-heavyweight title-holder.

French boxing fans may not have been exactly shouting from the top of the Eiffel Tower, or indeed dancing in the streets, but they must have been very pleased on 7 May 1977 when Lucien Rodriquez won the European heavyweight title by outpointing Belgium's Jean-Pierre Coopman over fifteen rounds in Antwerp. Rodriquez thus became the first French boxer to hold this crown since Battling Siki from Senegal (then a French colony), who reigned from 1922–3

Eva Shain put her name well and truly in the boxing record books on 29 September 1977 when she became the first female judge at a world heavy-weight title fight. The contest was Muhammad Ali's defence against the hard-hitting Earnie Shavers in New York, which was won by Ali on points over fifteen rounds.

Leon Spinks upset the odds and shocked fight experts on 15 February 1978 when he outpointed defending champion Muhammad Ali over fifteen rounds in Las Vegas to take the world heavyweight title. Spinks accomplished this feat in just his eighth professional

In February 1978 Leon Spinks provided a shock in just his eighth professional contest when he outpointed Muhammad Ali over fifteen rounds to win the world heavyweight title

contest – no other fighter in the division had ever won this crown with so few fights behind him.

During his career Ken Norton took part in three world heavyweight title fights and was defeated in each one of them – yet still he became a WBC world heavyweight champion. How?

Norton's first challenge was held on 26 March 1974 in Caracas, Venezuela, when he fought George Foreman and was stopped in round two.

Norton's second challenge came on 28 September 1976 in New York when Norton met defending champion Muhammad Ali and lost a fifteen-round points decision.

In Las Vegas, USA, on 5 November 1977, Norton met Jimmy Young in a final eliminator and won on a fifteen-round points decision. However, the then champion Leon Spinks defended *his* title against Muhammad Ali (whom he had previously beaten for the championship) rather than Norton. So the WBC stripped their version of the title from Spinks and made *Norton* their new champion.

Alas, Norton lost his crown in his first defence when outpointed over fifteen rounds by Larry Holmes in Las Vegas on 9 June 1978.

Muhammad Ali became the first man in the history of the sport to regain the world heavyweight title *twice* when he outpointed defending champion Leon Spinks over fifteen rounds on 15 September 1978 in New Orleans, USA. However, it should be noted that Ali only regained the WBA portion of the title since the WBC had stripped Spinks of their version of the title for his failure to defend against their number one contender Ken Norton.

After this victory over Spinks, Ali decided to call it a day and retired from the sport.

The Ali–Spinks return in 1978 really captured the fans' imagination since the encounter set another record at the time of having the highest indoor attendance (the total being 63,350).

During the 1979 world junior championships held in Yokohama, Japan, the gold medal at heavyweight went to the USA. The winner was Marvis Frazier – son of former world heavyweight champion Joe Frazier.

American Ray Patterson was a frequent visitor to British shores during his career, doing battle with some of the best home-grown fighters in the division at the time.

On 19 April 1966 Ray outpointed Carl Gizzi over ten rounds in London. Next, on 14 June 1966, Patterson halted Johnny Prescott in round five at Wembley. Patterson then lost a ten-round points decision in a return match with Carl Gizzi at Port Talbot, South Wales, on 12 July 1966.

Billy Gray was next to cross gloves with Patterson in Mayfair, London, on 8 September 1966, but after eight rounds a draw was given.

On 6 December 1966 Billy Walker then battled with the American at Kensington in London, punching his way to an exciting eight-round stoppage. At Wolverhampton, West Midlands, on 24 January 1967 Jack Bodell boxed his way to a ten-round points decision over Patterson.

Then Joe Bugner squared off against Patterson at Kensington in London on 21 April 1970, winning a decision on points over eight rounds.

Danny McAlinden was held to a draw over ten rounds at Wolverhampton by Patterson on 3 December 1970. At Mayfair in London on 20 November 1972, Richard Dunn won an eight-round points decision over Patterson. While Patterson may have lost more than he won, he always came to fight and would give fans real value for money while testing British fighters to the full.

Boxing talent clearly runs in the family since Ray was the younger brother of former two-time world heavyweight king Floyd Patterson.

Teófilo Stevenson of Cuba has the distinction of being the first heavyweight to win three gold medals at the Olympic Games. He won his medals at the following games:

★ Munich (1972)
★ Montreal (1976)
★ Moscow (1980)

Stevenson did not join the professional ranks, but many experts were of the opinion that, had he done so, he might well have won the world heavyweight title.

On 20 October 1979 in Pretoria, South Africa, Gerrie Coetzee became the first South African boxer to challenge for a version of the heavyweight championship. Coetzee fought American John Tate, who outpointed Coetzee over fifteen rounds to take the championship.

The 1979 Tate–Coetzee contest was the first world heavyweight title bout to take place in South Africa.

During his professional career Joe Bugner took part in more European heavyweight title fights than any other British boxer at the time. Joe was involved in nine of these title bouts, winning eight and losing one.

★★★ NINE TITLE BOUTS INVOLVING ★★★
★ JOE BUGNER ★

OPPONENT	RESULT FOR BUGNER	DATE
Henry Cooper	won title on points over 15 rounds	16 Mar 1971
Jurgen Blin	retained title on points over 15 rounds	11 May 1971
Jack Bodell	lost title on points over 15 rounds	27 Sep 1971
Jurgen Blin	regained title by an eight-round knockout	10 Oct 1972
Rudi Lubbers	retained title on points over 15 rounds	16 Jan 1973
Bepi Ros	retained title on points over 15 rounds	2 Oct 1973
Mario Baruzzi	retained title by nine-round retirement	29 May 1974
Dante Cane	retained title by four-round stoppage	1 Mar 1975
Richard Dunn	regained title by knockout in round one	12 Oct 1976

Joe Bugner participated in nine European heavyweight title bouts

Derek Rowe

CHAPTER SIX

MIKE TYSON'S REIGN

On 2 October 1980 in Las Vegas, USA, Muhammad Ali came out of retirement to challenge Larry Holmes for the WBC world heavyweight title. However, time had clearly caught up with Ali, who could not produce his skills of old, and so he retired from the contest in round ten.

This was the first time that Ali had ever been stopped in his professional career. Like so many champions before him, Muhammad had found that it is really difficult to come back successfully.

Frank Bruno won the ABA heavyweight championship in 1980, outpointing Rudi Pika over three rounds. In doing so, Bruno became at that time the youngest man in the history of the sport to win this title, being aged just eighteen years and six months.

On 30 March 1981, in a contest which took place in Birmingham, Gordon Ferris outpointed Billy Aird over fifteen rounds to capture the vacant British heavyweight crown. In so doing, Ferris became just the second Irish boxer since Danny McAlinden to hold this championship.

Joe Louis, one of the true greats of boxing, passed away on 12 April 1981. Whenever fans speak of boxing, his name is often mentioned.

Louis was born on 13 May 1914. During his career he fought a host of quality fighters, such as: Primo Carnera, Max Baer, Max Schmeling (twice), James J. Braddock, Tommy Farr, John Henry Lewis, Jack Sharkey, Jersey Joe Walcott (twice), Rocky Marciano, and Ezzard Charles.

In Halifax, Nova Scotia, on 21 July 1981, Trevor Berbick stopped Conroy Nelson for the Canadian and vacant Commonwealth heavyweight title in round two. Berbick became the first non-British heavyweight to hold the Commonwealth crown in this division since Jamaica's Joe Bygraves, who had lost the title to Joe Erskine by way of a fifteen-round points decision on 25 November 1957.

Trevor Berbick had been born in Jamaica, but had held Canadian nationality.

On 12 October 1981 future British heavyweight champion David Pearce won a contest that could be considered one of his best ever victories during his professional career. In Bloomsbury, London, he stopped opponent Dennis Andries in round seven. Andries was later to go on and punch his way to the British light-heavyweight title, win the WBC world light-heavyweight crown on three separate occasions, and capture the British cruiserweight championship.

It must have been a nightmare for TV commentators when two boxers with the same surname fought each other in France on 26 November 1981 for the vacant European heavyweight title. The boxers concerned were former European title-holder Lucien Rodriguez of France and Felipe Rodriguez of Spain. Lucien won a twelve-round points decision to capture the championship.

Former world heavyweight champion Joe Frazier made a ring comeback on 3 December 1981 in Chicago, when he fought a ten-round draw against Floyd Cummings. Alas, it was clear from this performance that Frazier's best fighting days were behind him, and it proved to be his last contest. Frazier's professional record was thirty-seven bouts, winning thirty-two with four defeats and only one draw.

On 11 December 1981 in Nassau, The Bahamas, Muhammad Ali lost a ten-round points decision to Canadian Trevor Berbick in what was to be Ali's final professional contest. Ali, the former three-time heavyweight champion of the world, was but a mere shadow of the former fighter who had once left the fans amazed by his boxing skills. Nevertheless, Ali's name will always linked with the greats of the division.

Ali left boxing with a professional record of sixty-one bouts, winning fifty-six and losing just five.

During his professional career Muhammad Ali went the full distance of fifteen rounds in world heavyweight title fights more often than any previous champion at that time.

Derek Rowe

Muhammad Ali had his last contest on 11 December 1981, when he was outpointed by Trevor Berbick over ten rounds

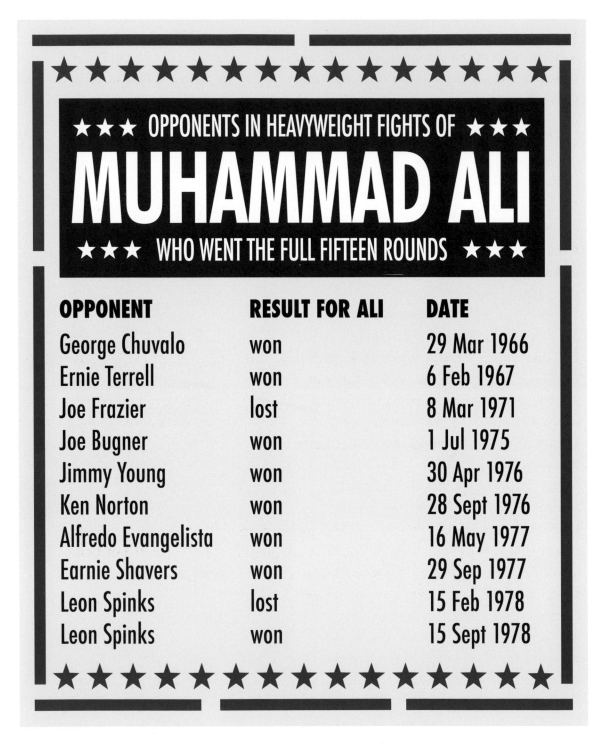

★★★ OPPONENTS IN HEAVYWEIGHT FIGHTS OF ★★★
MUHAMMAD ALI
★★★ WHO WENT THE FULL FIFTEEN ROUNDS ★★★

OPPONENT	RESULT FOR ALI	DATE
George Chuvalo	won	29 Mar 1966
Ernie Terrell	won	6 Feb 1967
Joe Frazier	lost	8 Mar 1971
Joe Bugner	won	1 Jul 1975
Jimmy Young	won	30 Apr 1976
Ken Norton	won	28 Sept 1976
Alfredo Evangelista	won	16 May 1977
Earnie Shavers	won	29 Sep 1977
Leon Spinks	lost	15 Feb 1978
Leon Spinks	won	15 Sept 1978

During his professional career Muhammad Ali fought four Olympic Gold medal winners in world title bouts: Floyd Patterson, who won gold at middleweight in 1952; Joe Frazier, who won gold at heavyweight in 1964; George Foreman, who won gold at heavyweight in 1968; and Leon Spinks, who won gold at light-heavyweight in 1976.

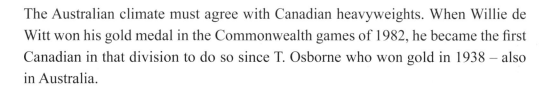

The Australian climate must agree with Canadian heavyweights. When Willie de Witt won his gold medal in the Commonwealth games of 1982, he became the first Canadian in that division to do so since T. Osborne who won gold in 1938 – also in Australia.

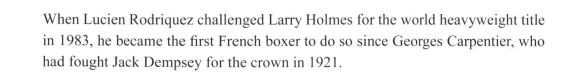

On 22 January 1983 South African Gerrie Coetzee met American Pinklon Thomas in Atlantic City, USA. The bout was declared a draw after ten rounds.

In the course of time both boxers were to go on and win a version of the world title. Coetzee won the WBA title in 1983, and Thomas won the WBC crown in 1984. But never again did the two meet inside a ring.

Larry Holmes defended his WBC world crown on 27 March 1983, boxing his way to a twelve-round points decision over Lucien Rodriquez of France in a contest staged in Scranton, USA. This was the first WBC heavyweight title bout to be scheduled for twelve rounds rather than fifteen.

When Lucien Rodriquez challenged Larry Holmes for the world heavyweight title in 1983, he became the first French boxer to do so since Georges Carpentier, who had fought Jack Dempsey for the crown in 1921.

It was a case of 'so near, yet so far' for Mike Weaver, who almost became the third man to regain the world heavyweight championship when he drew with defending WBA title-holder Michael Dokes over fifteen rounds on 20 May 1983 in Las Vegas. Weaver had previously lost the crown to Dokes on 10 December 1982 (also in Las Vegas) when he was stopped at the sixty-third second of the first round.

Briton Joe Bugner lost a twelve-round points decision when he fought former world heavyweight champion Joe Frazier on 2 July 1973 in England. So it was going to be interesting to see how Marvis Frazier, Joe Frazier's son, would fare against the same man in Atlantic City, USA, on 4 June 1983.

Actually, it proved to be a double for the Frazier family when Marvis emulated his father by outpointing the former British, European and Commonwealth heavyweight champion over ten rounds.

On 22 September 1983 David Pearce won the British heavyweight championship when he stopped defending title-holder Neville Meade in round nine. The bout staged in Cardiff was an historic occasion since this was the last British championship contest at the weight to be scheduled for fifteen rounds. In future all British title bouts would be held over the duration of twelve rounds.

Gerrie Coetzee of South Africa became the first white heavyweight to win a version of the world heavyweight title since Ingemar Johansson when he knocked out WBA title-holder Michael Dokes in round ten on 23 September 1983 in Richfield, USA.

This was third time lucky for Coetzee for he had failed in two previous attempts to win the championship. Coetzee had first challenged for the title on 20 October 1979 in Pretoria, South Africa, when he had been outpointed over fifteen rounds for the vacant crown by American John Tate. His second bid had come on 25

October 1980 in Sun City, South Africa, against another American fighter, Mike Weaver, who won by a knockout in round thirteen.

During 1983 Larry Holmes relinquished the WBC version of the world heavyweight title and accepted recognition by the newly formed IBF as world champion. In so doing Larry became the first heavyweight to be given sole recognition by this then fledging organization.

Shock waves shook British boxing on 13 May 1984 when American James Smith knocked out British hope Frank Bruno in round ten at Wembley.

Many experts had felt that Bruno, who had gone into this contest with an undefeated record of twenty-one bouts, could eventually go all the way to the top, and thus had a very real chance of being the first British boxer to win the world heavyweight title since Bob Fitzsimmons. Now British fans had to think again after this result.

Norway produced its first European heavyweight champion on 9 November 1984 when Steffen Tangstad outpointed holder Lucien Rodriguez of France over twelve rounds in Denmark.

Nigel Benn (left) and Frank Bruno enjoy a night at the British Boxing Board of Control Awards ceremony

American Greg Page won the WBA heavyweight crown in Sun City, South Africa, when he knocked out the defending champion Gerrie Coetzee in eight rounds on 1 December 1984. However, Greg was lucky to be given a shot at the title in the first place since he had lost his previous two bouts. On 9 March 1984 he lost a twelve-round points decision when he fought Tim Witherspoon for the vacant WBC championship in Las Vegas. Then, on 31 August 1984 Page defended his United States Boxing Association (USBA) title against David Bey in Las Vegas, and once again lost a twelve-round points decision.

Mike Tyson made his professional debut in 1985, defeating Hector Mercedes

When Greg Page won the WBA heavyweight title he became at that time the fourth man from Kentucky to win a version of the heavyweight title. The previous three title-holders from Kentucky were: Marvin Hart, Muhammad Ali and Jimmy Ellis.

Mike Tyson made his professional debut on 6 March 1985, blasting out opponent Hector Mercedes from Puerto Rico in the first round in New York.

In 1985 Tyson proved to be a busy fighter, boxing fifteen times in all and winning every contest inside the scheduled distance, with eleven bouts finishing in the first round. The message was clear: Tyson was not just a new kid on the block, but also an outstanding prospect with chilling knockout power in his fists.

When, on 9 March 1985, Anders Eklund stopped Norway's defending European heavyweight champion Steffen Tangstad in four rounds in Copenhagen, Denmark, he became the first boxer from Sweden to win this title since Ingemar Johansson (who had held the title twice from 1956–9 and then from 1962–3).

Hughroy Currie won the vacant British heavyweight title on 18 September 1985, outpointing opponent Funso Banjo over twelve rounds at the Alexandra Pavilion in London. This was the first championship contest at the weight to be staged over twelve rounds.

In Las Vegas, USA, on 21 September 1985, Michael Spinks outpointed holder Larry Holmes over fifteen rounds for the IBF version of the world heavyweight title. With his victory, Spinks became the first world light-heavyweight king to win this crown.

It should be noted that when Michael Spinks defeated Larry Holmes in September 1985 there was an element of revenge. On 12 June 1981 Holmes had stopped Michael's brother Leon in three rounds when defending his WBC title (Leon being a former world champion at the time).

Derek Rowe

In 1985 Frank Bruno won the European heavyweight title by knocking out holder Anders Eklund in the fourth round

Michael and Leon Spinks were the first brothers to hold the world heavyweight championship of the world, with Michael winning in 1985 and Leon in 1978.

When Larry Holmes lost his IBF world heavyweight crown to Michael Spinks he also lost his chance to equal Rocky Marciano's record of being undefeated in forty-nine professional contests.

Frank Bruno won his first major title in the professional ranks when he challenged Anders Eklund of Sweden for the European title at Wembley on 1 October 1985. Bruno later relinquished the championship without making a defence so that he could concentrate on working his way towards a shot at the world title.

Future British and Commonwealth heavyweight champion Horace Notice scored an excellent win when he outpointed Anaclet Wamba of France over eight rounds in Kensington, London, on 16 October 1985. It was only Notice's eighth contest. It could be argued that it was his best ever victory.

Wamba later went on to win the European title and WBC version of the world cruiserweight title.

Tim Witherspoon, the third man to regain a world heavyweight crown

Les Clark

Tim Witherspoon became the third man to regain the world heavyweight title when he outpointed holder Tony Tubbs over fifteen rounds for the WBA version of the championship in Atlanta, Georgia, on 17 January 1986.

Witherspoon had previously held the WBC portion of the title, but duly lost the crown on 31 August 1984 when he was outpointed over twelve rounds in Las Vegas by Pinklon Thomas.

Frank Bruno knocked out former WBA world heavyweight champion Gerrie Coetzee of South Africa in the first round at Wembley on 4 March 1986. At the time, this was the best victory by Bruno in the professional ranks.

For the first time since Tommy Burns reigned from 1906–8, Canada had a world heavyweight champion in the shape of Trevor Berbick, who pulled off a surprise by outpointing defending American WBC title-holder Pinklon Thomas over twelve rounds in Las Vegas on 22 March 1986.

On 22 March 1986 Dwight Muhammad Qawi retained his WBA world cruiser-weight title in Reno, USA, when he stopped Leon Spinks in round six. On this occasion Spinks became the first former world heavyweight champion to drop down a division to challenge for this crown.

On 12 April 1986 Horace Notice won the British heavyweight title and vacant Commonwealth crown when he stopped Hughroy Currie in the sixth round. This was the first time that a British heavyweight title had been contested on the Isle of Man.

On 19 April 1986 Larry Holmes failed in Las Vegas to regain his IBF title from holder Michael Spinks when he was outpointed over fifteen rounds. This proved to be the last world heavyweight title fight to go the full fifteen rounds.

Mike Tyson had won all his previous nineteen bouts inside the distance without any problems. The punching power of Tyson was spectacular. However, on 3 May 1986 in New York, opponent James Tillis, a former world heavyweight title challenger, used his ring experience to put a halt to Tyson's quick wins by lasting the distance – only to lose on a ten-round points decision to the undefeated Tyson.

Frank Bruno (left) and commentator Harry Carpenter getting together one evening

Les Clark

On 19 July 1986 Frank Bruno became the first British heavyweight since Brian London to challenge for the world crown on home turf. (London had challenged Muhammad Ali in England on 6 August 1966 and had been knocked out in the third round.)

Bruno gave it all he had, but was unable to bring the crown to Britain when ring-wise defending title-holder Tim Witherspoon retained his title by stopping Bruno in round eleven at Wembley.

It should also be noted that in the same match Bruno became the first British heavyweight to challenge for the WBA's version of the championship.

Many fans watched with keen anticipation when hard-hitting Mike Tyson met Marvis Frazier (the son of Joe Frazier) in New York on 26 July 1986. However, the powerful Tyson made short work of his opponent, stopping him in the first round to score his fifteenth victory in the opening round, and thus taking his undefeated record to twenty-five not out.

Many that night must have wondered what would have happened had Mike Tyson and Joe Frazier boxed in the same era. How explosive an encounter would it have been, with their respective aggressive, come-forward styles? Such a prospect really is the stuff dream fights are made of!

On 6 September 1986 Steffen Tangstad became the first boxer from Norway to challenge for the world heavyweight title. However, he failed to become the first man from his country to win the crown when defending IBF king Michael Spinks ended both his hopes and dreams by stopping him in round four in Las Vegas.

By stopping title-holder Trevor Berbick of Canada in two sensational rounds in Las Vegas on 22 November 1986, Mike Tyson punched his way to the WBC heavyweight title.

Tyson really looked something special in this bout; the experienced champion Berbick just could not stand up to the power of his challenging punches. Thus, Tyson became, at the age of twenty years, four months and twenty-three days, the youngest man at that point to win the championship, and he was now undefeated in twenty-eight professional contests.

On 12 December 1986 James Smith caused an upset when he stopped defending champion Tim Witherspoon in the first round in New York to win the WBA world heavyweight title. Britain's Frank Bruno must have had more than a mild interest in this contest, since both Smith and Witherspoon had defeated him in previous bouts.

On 7 March 1987 Mike Tyson, the WBC title-holder, and James Smith, the WBA champion, met in a unification contest in Las Vegas. At the end of the twelve-round encounter, Tyson emerged the victor on points to claim another version of the championship, putting the division one step closer to having an undisputed world champion.

Former world heavyweight champion George Foreman made his comeback to professional boxing on 9 March 1987 in Sacramento, USA, when he stopped Steve Zouski in four rounds.

Les Clark

Former world heavyweight champion George Foreman made a ring comeback in 1987

Prior to this contest, Foreman's last ring appearance had been on 17 March 1977, when opponent Jimmy Young outpointed him over twelve rounds in San Juan.

On 30 May 1987 in Las Vegas, USA, Tony Tucker won the vacant IBF version of the world heavyweight crown when he stopped James Douglas in round ten for the championship. In so doing, Tucker became the third boxer to hold this version of the title following Larry Holmes and Michael Spinks.

On 1 August 1987 WBC and WBA world heavyweight champion Mike Tyson outpointed IBF holder Tony Tucker over twelve rounds in Las Vegas to become the first undisputed king of the division since Leon Spinks, who had outpointed Muhammad Ali over fifteen rounds in February 1978.

Soon after that contest, Spinks was stripped of the WBC crown because he fought Muhammad Ali in a return bout rather than meet the WBC's number one contender, Ken Norton. This left Spinks with just the WBA championship. The titles remained split until Tyson and Tucker fought in 1987.

When Tony Tucker lost the IBF version of the world crown to Mike Tyson in 1987, he became the fighter who held the title for the shortest period of time in the history of the sport at that time. Tucker had won the championship on 30 May 1987 and lost it to Tyson on 1 August 1987 – a period of just two months and two days.

On 29 August 1987 middleweight Mark Holmes outpointed opponent Jerome Kelly over ten rounds in Pennsylvania, USA. This proved to be Holmes' last contest.

He left the game with an impressive professional record of thirty-eight wins in thirty-nine bouts.

His older brother, however, was an even harder act to follow since he was Larry Holmes, the former WBC and IBF heavyweight champion.

On 6 October 1987 the then former WBC world and British light-heavyweight champion Dennis Andries outpointed Robert Folley over ten rounds in Arizona, USA. The heavyweight connection here is that Robert was the son of the late Zora Folley, a once highly ranked and well-respected heavyweight contender who had challenged Muhammad Ali for the world heavyweight title in March 1967. However, Zora Folley had failed to take the crown when knocked out in round seven by Ali.

Italian Francesco Damiani punched his way to the European heavyweight title on 9 October 1987 when he stopped title-holder Anders Eklund of Sweden in six rounds in Aosta, Italy.

Damiani, who won a silver medal at super-heavyweight at the 1984 Olympic Games in Los Angeles, was now undefeated in nineteen professional bouts.

On 16 October 1987 Mike Tyson defended his world heavyweight title against fellow American Tyrell Biggs in Atlantic City, USA. Both boxers came into the ring with undefeated records: Biggs having a perfect slate of fifteen victories *and* being a former 1984 Olympic gold medal winner at super heavyweight; Tyson having a record of thirty-one winning bouts.

In the event, it was Biggs who suffered the first defeat in the professional ring when Tyson retained his championship by way of a seven-round stoppage. This was the last world heavyweight championship contest to be scheduled for fifteen rounds.

When Horace Notice knocked out Paul Lister in three rounds in defence of his British and Commonwealth titles on 3 November 1987 in Sunderland, Tyne & Wear, he became the first champion since Henry Cooper to win a Lonsdale Belt outright.

After Cooper, the following men held the title. Joe Bugner (who, of course, defeated Cooper); Jack Bodell; Danny McAlinden; Bunny Johnson; Richard Dunn; Joe Bugner (who regained the title); John L. Gardner; Gordon Ferris; Neville Meade; David Pearce; and Hughroy Currie.

On 22 January 1988 Larry Holmes came out of retirement in Atlantic City, USA, to challenge Mike Tyson for the world heavyweight title. However, Holmes was unable to defuse the dynamite in the gloved fists of the champion and failed to regain the crown when he was stopped in round four. Tyson thus became the first man in the professional ranks to stop Holmes inside the distance.

On 9 March 1988 Horace Notice retained his British and Commonwealth heavyweight titles when he stopped Hughroy Currie in round ten in a contest which took place at York Hall in London. This proved to be to Notice's last professional bout since he was later forced to retire due to a detached retina. However, Notice has the distinction of being the first holder of the British heavyweight title to retire with an undefeated record.

Horace Notice had sixteen bouts, winning twelve inside the distance.

When Mike Tyson stopped former WBA heavyweight king Tony Tubbs in two rounds in defence of his world heavyweight title on 21 March 1988, it marked the first time that Tyson had fought outside the USA during his time in the professional ranks. The contest took place in Tokyo, Japan.

On 30 March 1988 former WBA world heavyweight champion John Tate had his first professional contest in England at the York Hall, London. His opponent was Noel Quarless from Liverpool. The American had won his last fourteen bouts in a row and was expected to add Quarless to his victory list. However, on the night Quarless produced a shock to defeat Tate by way of a ten-round points decision.

There was very little doubt that at the time Mike Tyson ruled the roost at heavyweight as the undisputed champion, holding the WBC, WBA and IBF titles. No man could stand in his way except perhaps one fighter: Michael Spinks, the former undisputed world light-heavyweight king and IBF world heavyweight champion.

The two met on 27 June 1988 in Atlantic City, USA. A long battle was expected between the two. However, once again Tyson proved his right to the heavyweight throne by knocking out Spinks in just the first round.

Frank Bruno challenged Mike Tyson for the world heavyweight title on 25 February 1989 in Las Vegas. This was Bruno's first contest since stopping Joe Bugner in eight rounds on 24 October 1987. However, Frank failed to lift the championship when stopped in round five.

Frank was just the second British boxer to challenge twice for this title since Brian London, and also the first since London to contest the heavyweight crown in America.

On 19 July 1986 Tim Witherspoon had stopped Bruno in round eleven; Floyd Patterson had knocked out Brian London in round eleven on 1 May 1959 (in Indianapolis, USA); and Muhammad Ali had knocked out London in three rounds on 6 August 1966 (in England).

Lennox pictured during a sparring session wearing a headguard to reduce the risk of facial damage

Les Clark

On 16 March 1989 former European heavyweight champion Anders Eklund from Sweden came in as a late substitute for Columbian Bernardo Mercado and outpointed American Philipp Brown over twelve rounds in Nevada, USA, to win the vacant World Boxing Americas heavyweight title. By this victory Eklund earned the distinction of being the first European heavyweight boxer to capture this crown.

It was a case of '*Mamma Mia*, he's a champ!' when Italy's Francesco Damiani of Italy became the first holder of the WBO world heavyweight title on knocking out South African Johnny Du Plooy in three rounds. The contest took place on 6 May 1989 in Syracuse, Sicilia, Italy. Damiani thus became the first Italian heavyweight to hold a version of the title since Primo Carnera, who had held the title from 1933–4.

On 27 June 1989 Lennox Lewis, a man who was set to take British heavyweight boxing into a golden era, made his professional debut in Kensington, London, knocking out Al Malcolm in round two. Lewis – who was born in Britain, but emigrated to Canada at a young age – later developed into an excellent boxer in the amateur ranks, winning for his adopted country gold medals at super-heavyweight in the 1986 Commonwealth Games and at 1988 Olympic Games. However, Lennox later returned to his country of birth in his bid for world professional honours.

On 5 December 1989 Derek Williams stopped Hughroy Currie in fifty-five seconds of the first round to win the vacant European heavyweight championship. The contest took place in Brockley, London, where Williams was also defending his Commonwealth crown.

This was the first all-British European heavyweight title fight since 12 October 1976, when Richard Dunn defended his European crown along with his British and Commonwealth titles against Joe Bugner.

It is ironic to note that this contest also ended in the opening round with Bugner regaining his titles by a knockout. The Williams–Currie bout was also the first time that two British boxers had contested a vacant European heavyweight title contest since Henry Cooper outpointed Brian London over fifteen rounds on 24 February 1964.

CHAPTER SEVEN

LENNOX LEWIS: KING OF THE WORLD

When Mike Tyson defended his world heavyweight title against challenger James Douglas in Japan on 11 February 1990, few – if any – gave Douglas a chance of victory. The smart money was well and truly on a Tyson victory. Even so, the challenger turned the form book not only upside-down but inside-out by knocking out the champion in round ten – and this after Douglas had been floored in round eight.

However, there was a degree of controversy about the victory since it was claimed Douglas was on the canvas longer than ten seconds in round eight. Despite this, the decision duly stood and Douglas left Tokyo as the new champion and the man who had produced the biggest shock in boxing for many years.

Knut Blin won the German International heavyweight title in Hamburg on 16 November 1990 when he stopped Mario Guedes in round seven. Knut was the son of former European heavyweight champion Jurgen Blin.

On 25 September 1990 former world heavyweight champion George Foreman made his professional debut in England where he met fellow American Terry Anderson at Millwall. The fans did not get much of an opportunity to appreciate Foreman's skill, since his powerful punches soon found the target zone and he knocked out Anderson in the first round.

On 25 October 1990 Evander Holyfield made history in Las Vegas when he became the first former world cruiserweight champion to win the world heavyweight crown.

To win, Holyfield knocked out title-holder James Douglas in the third round. Douglas had been making the first defence of the title that he had taken in sensational fashion from Mike Tyson earlier that year.

Lennox Lewis made his professional debut on the 27 June 1989 when he knocked out Al Malcolm in two rounds

Les Clark

Lennox Lewis sent out the message that he was for real on 31 October 1990 by winning his first professional title in his fourteenth contest. Lewis stopped title-holder Jean Chanet of France at Crystal Palace, London, in six rounds to win the European heavyweight title.

On 11 January 1991 Ray Mercer (heavyweight gold medal winner at the 1988 Olympic Games) became the first American holder of the WBO world heavyweight title in Atlantic City when he punched his way to victory in dramatic fashion by knocking out Italian title-holder Francesco Damiani in round nine.

On 2 March 1991 two American boxers Mike Evans and former IBF world cruiserweight king Lee Roy Murphy met at Darlington, County Durham, to contest the vacant IBF Inter-Continental heavyweight title. Evans took the crown with a twelve-round points decision. This was the first time that this title had been contested in England.

On 6 March 1991 British champion Gary Mason and European title-holder Lennox Lewis faced their moment of truth at Wembley when they met in defence of their respective titles. Both men had yet to lose in the professional ranks, Mason being undefeated in thirty-five fights and Lewis fourteen. Alas, one man had to lose his perfect record and this proved to be Mason, who was stopped in round seven with his right eye closed.

In this bout Lewis became the first Olympic gold medal winner to win the British heavyweight championship.

On 19 April 1991 former world heavyweight champion George Foreman, aged forty-two years, three months and nine days, challenged Evander Holyfield in Atlantic City, USA, for the world heavyweight title. While Foreman may have lost on a twelve-round points decision to the defending champion, Foreman kept his pride and dignity and proved that even at an advanced age he was still more than a worthy challenger and not a fighter to underrate.

On 30 September 1991 Glenn McCrory became the first former holder of the British cruiserweight title to challenge for the British heavyweight championship, but failed in his bid to win the crown at Kensington, London, when knocked out by holder Lennox Lewis in round two.

Lewis was also defending his European crown against McCrory, who was also a former IBF world and Commonwealth cruiserweight champion.

On 12 November 1991 J. A. Bugner made his professional debut, outpointing opponent Denroy Bryan over the duration of four rounds at Milton Keynes, England.

Bugner was the son of former British, European and Commonwealth heavyweight champion Joe Bugner. While the younger Bugner showed undoubted skill, he failed to duplicate his father's title-winning success during the course of his boxing career, winning nine while drawing one and losing two of his bouts.

'Revenge is sweet' or so it is often said. Well, if that is true, then Lennox Lewis must have been full of honey when he fought American Tyrell Biggs in Atlanta, Georgia, on 23 November 1991, duly stopping Biggs in three rounds. In the 1984 Olympic quarterfinals, Biggs had defeated Lewis and had gone on to capture gold at super-heavyweight. With this 1991 win, Lewis had now put the record straight and avenged that loss, confirming also that he was a heavyweight heading for the very top of the division.

In Norwich, Norfolk, on 21 January 1992, Herbie Hide stopped opponent Conroy Nelson of Canada in two rounds to capture the vacant WBC International heavyweight title. In so doing, he became the first British boxer in the division to hold this crown.

Les Clark

Herbie Hide with his WBO world title belt

On 7 February 1992 Larry Holmes outpointed Ray Mercer over twelve rounds in Atlantic City, USA. Prior to this contest Mercer had relinquished his WBO heavyweight title, since he chose to fight Holmes rather than the number one contender Michael Moorer. Had Mercer still been champion Holmes would have once again been wearing a version of the world heavyweight crown. However, by this victory Larry proved that he was still a threat in the division and should not be taken lightly by other contenders.

On 30 April 1992 at Kensington, London, Lennox Lewis defended his British and European heavyweight titles against Derek Williams, who also had his Commonwealth crown at stake. Lewis won his third championship when he stopped Williams in round three. Since Lewis had now secured three British title victories, he won the Lonsdale belt outright.

It has often been said that there is a first time for everything in life – well, that was most certainly true on 15 May 1992 in Atlantic City, USA, when Michael Moorer won the vacant WBO world heavyweight title, stopping fellow American Bert Cooper in five rounds.

With this victory, Moorer became the first boxer with the southpaw stance to win a version of the world heavyweight championship.

In Albany, New York, on 23 June 1992, Tracy Harris Patterson won the WBC World Super-bantamweight title by stopping defending champion Thierry Jacob of France in two rounds.

Tracy was the adopted son of former two-time world heavyweight champion Floyd Patterson, so by this victory Tracy was able to emulate his father in winning a world crown.

At Earls Court, London, on 31 October 1992, Lennox Lewis made the sporting world sit up and really take interest when he scored a sensational win by stopping highly ranked contender Donovan 'Razor' Ruddock in two rounds.

The contest was a final eliminator for the WBC world heavyweight title with Lewis' Commonwealth crown also at stake. At the time the victory was considered to be the finest for many years by a British heavyweight over a top fighter in the division.

On 13 November 1992 in Las Vegas, USA, Riddick Bowe outpointed defending champion Evander Holyfield over twelve rounds to win the world heavyweight title. In so doing, Bowe became the first man to defeat Holyfield in the professional ranks. Going into the contest Holyfield was undefeated in twenty-eight bouts and Bowe undefeated in thirty-one.

The IBO saw its first heavyweight champion crowned when former WBC world heavyweight title-holder Pinklon Thomas outpointed fellow American Craig Payne over twelve rounds on 14 November 1992 to take the vacant championship in South Carolina, USA.

In December 1992 Lennox Lewis won the world heavyweight title without throwing a punch when he was awarded the championship by the World Boxing Council (WBC). This situation came about when agreement could not be reached for a Riddick Bowe defence against Lewis. Bowe, however, retained the WBA and IBF portions of the crown. The long wait for a British world heavyweight king was now over (the last British champion at this weight had been Bob Fitzsimmons, who had won the title in 1897 and lost it in 1899).

Derek Rowe

Lennox Lewis was proclaimed the world heavyweight champion by the WBC when Riddick Bowe relinquished that version of the title

With Lennox Lewis becoming the WBC world heavyweight king, some glory was also due to his manager, Frank Maloney, as the first British manager to take his charge to the supreme championship.

When Lennox Lewis acquired the WBC world heavyweight championship in 1992, he became the first Olympic gold medallist at the super-heavyweight poundage to hold this crown.

On 29 January 1993 American Lawrence Carter became the first holder of the WBF heavyweight title in South Carolina, USA, when he stopped fellow countryman and former WBC world heavyweight champion, Pinklon Thomas, in round seven.

In his thirty-ninth bout, Frank Bruno stopped American Carl 'The Truth' Williams in the tenth round. The bout was fought at the National Exhibition Centre in Birmingham on 24 April 1993.

Surprisingly, this was the first time that Bruno had fought on British soil outside London during his professional career.

When Henry Akinwande outpointed Axel Schulz over twelve rounds in Berlin on 1 May 1993, he took the vacant European heavyweight title, thus becoming the first British boxer since Dick Richardson to win a European heavyweight title bout in Germany.

In that earlier contest, which had been fought in Dortmund on 24 February 1962, Richardson had defended his crown against challenger Karl Mildenberger. Richardson ended the match with a knockout in the first round.

On 8 May 1993 at the Thomas & Mack Center in Las Vegas, Lennox Lewis made the first defence of his WBC world heavyweight title. Lewis outpointed American challenger and former IBF king Tony Tucker over twelve rounds.

Thus, Lewis became the first British-born heavyweight since Bob Fitzsimmons to win a world heavyweight title fight in the USA. In 1897 Fitzsimmons had defeated James J. Corbett, so it would not be an understatement to say that, from a British point of view, such a victory was long overdue.

On 22 May 1993, Riddick Bowe, who was making the second defence of his WBA world heavyweight title, stopped challenger Jesse Ferguson in two rounds. It is quite incredible to note that this was the first world heavyweight championship bout to be held in Washington DC for over fifty years – the last being the Louis–Baer bout on 23 May 1941, when Louis retained his crown following Baer's disqualification in round seven.

The IBF refused to sanction the 1993 Bowe–Ferguson contest because Ferguson was not ranked in the IBF ratings.

The Bowe–Ferguson world title contest proved to be something of a milestone since for the first time in the history of the sport not one, but three, lady judges officiated: Sheila Harmon-Martin, Patricia Jarman and Eugenia Williams.

On 7 June 1993 Tommy Morrison outpointed former world heavyweight champion George Foreman over twelve rounds in Las Vegas to win the vacant WBO world heavyweight title. In so doing, Morrison became the first white American to hold a version of the world heavyweight title since Rocky Marciano.

When Tommy Morrison won the WBO world heavyweight title it was like life imitating art since previously Morrison had appeared in the movie *Rocky V* with actor Sylvester Stallone. In the film, Morrison's character is Tommy Gunn, a boxer who also wins the world heavyweight crown.

Les Clark

Lennox Lewis and Frank Bruno made history when they became the first British fighters to meet each other in a world heavyweight title contest

Boxing history was made on 1 October 1993 when the first ever all-British world heavyweight championship bout took place between defending title-holder Lennox Lewis and challenger Frank Bruno at Cardiff Arms Park – the first world heavyweight title contest ever to be staged in Wales.

Lewis retained his crown when the referee stopped the contest in round seven. Although Bruno had failed in his ultimate aim, he did create a record of being the first Briton to challenge unsuccessfully on three occasions for this highly respected championship.

Mickey Vann put his name in the record books on the night in question by being the first referee to handle a world heavyweight championship between two British boxers (Lennox Lewis and Frank Bruno).

On 29 October 1993, American Michael Bentt upset the odds when he stopped defending champion Tommy Morrison in the first round to win the WBO heavyweight title in Tulsa, Oklahoma. In so doing, Bentt became the third British-born boxer to win a version of the title, for, although now representing the USA, he had been born in Britain.

The two other British-born boxers who had held this title were Bob Fitzsimmons and Lennox Lewis.

On 6 November 1993, Evander Holyfield challenged Riddick Bowe for the WBA and IBF versions of the world heavyweight title in Las Vegas, and thus Holyfield became just the fourth man in the history of the division to regain the championship. At the end of the twelve-round contest, Holyfield became the first man to defeat Bowe when he was given the decision on points. Going into the contest, Bowe had been undefeated in thirty-four bouts.

Previous boxers to regain the title are as follows: Floyd Patterson, Muhammad Ali and Tim Witherspoon – Witherspoon had won the WBA version of the championship after previously holding the WBC crown.

During the Holyfield–Bowe encounter it would not have been out of place if someone had shouted 'Is it a bird? Is it a plane?' when someone came flying down towards the ring as the action was taking place.

No, it was not Superman, but a parasailer by the name of James Miller, who landed on the ropes and then proceeded to hold up the contest for just over twenty minutes.

Les Clark

Herbie Hide, seen here with his collection of championship belts, won the WBO world heavyweight crown on 19 March 1994, stopping title-holder Michael Bentt in seven rounds

On 19 March 1994, British title-holder Herbie Hide won the WBO version of the world heavyweight crown when he knocked out defending champion Michael Bentt in seven rounds at Millwall in London. At that particular moment in time British heavyweight boxing was on a high, since there were now two Britons holding world heavyweight titles (the other champion being, of course, WBC king Lennox Lewis).

A new record was duly created when Herbie Hide captured the WBO version of the world crown for it was the first time that two successive holders of the British heavyweight title had gone on to win versions of the heavyweight championship of the world.

On 22 April 1994 in Las Vegas, USA, Michael Moorer became the first boxer with the southpaw stance to hold versions of the WBA and IBF world heavyweight championships when he outpointed defending champion Evander Holyfield over twelve rounds.

Moorer was a former holder of the WBO world heavyweight title (and the first southpaw holder of this championship).

In Bristol, England, on 25 May 1994, Julius Francis was knocked out in four rounds by Latino boxer John Ruiz. Nevertheless, in time both fighters would go on to become champions: Francis, a British and Commonwealth title-holder at heavy-weight; and Ruiz, a WBA world heavyweight king.

On 24 September 1994 Lennox Lewis became a fighter involved in a fight of four firsts. Lewis became the first British world heavyweight champion (WBC version) to defend his title in England when he met American challenger Oliver McCall at Wembley in a contest he was clearly expected to win. Certainly the fighter from the USA was worthy of a shot at the championship, but Lewis was considered to be a far better ring operator in every department. However, on the night, McCall became the first man to defeat Lewis in the professional ranks (stopping him in the second round), the first to put him on the canvas, and the first to stop him inside the distance. All in all, it was a very bad night for Lewis and British boxing in general.

Les Clark

In 1994 Oliver McCall did the unexpected and stopped defending champion Lennox Lewis in two rounds to win the WBC world heavyweight title

In Las Vegas on 5 November 1994 George Foreman became the oldest man at that time to win the world heavyweight championship (both WBA and IBF versions) when he knocked out title-holder Michael Moorer in ten rounds.

At the time of the fight, Foreman was aged forty-five years, nine months and twenty-six days.

Here's a thought! Michael Moorer was born on 12 November 1967. George Foreman had his first professional contest on 23 June 1969. While Foreman was learning the boxing trade, Moorer must have been learning to walk and talk.

A new record, which could be called a bit of a tall order, was created in Cardiff, Wales, on 19 November 1994 when James Oyebola knocked out Clifton Mitchell in the fourth round, thus retaining his WBC International heavyweight title and winning the vacant British crown.

At this time Oyebola became the tallest man to hold the British heavyweight championship, being at the listed height of 6 ft 9 in.

When James Oyebola won the British heavyweight championship in 1994, he became the first former holder of the ABA Super-heavyweight title to do so. Oyebola won his ABA titles in 1986 and 1987.

American Riddick Bowe won the WBO version of the crown when he knocked out Britain's defending title-holder Herbie Hide in round six in Las Vegas on 11 March 1995.

At that moment Bowe became the first heavyweight to have held all four major versions of the world heavyweight title (the previous versions being the WBC, WBA and IBF).

In November 1994 James Oyebola became the tallest man to hold a heavyweight crown

American heavyweight Ron Lyle, who was born on 12 February 1941, was a top class fighter during his professional career, fighting such boxers as Jerry Quarry, Oscar Bonavena, Jimmy Young (twice), Jimmy Ellis, Buster Mathis, Earnie Shavers, George Foreman, and Joe Bugner. Lyle even challenged Muhammad Ali for the world heavyweight title in Las Vegas on 16 May 1975, but was stopped in round eleven.

The curtain appeared to come down on his boxing career when he was knocked out in round one by Gerry Cooney on 24 October 1980. However, to everyone's surprise, Lyle returned to the ring on 7 April 1995, while in his fifty-fourth year. The

Zeljko Mavrovic became the first boxer from Croatia to win the European heavyweight title

Les Clark

contest, which took place in Kentucky, USA, saw Ron, who was clearly young at heart, knock out opponent Bruce Johnson in round four.

Ron had three more winning bouts that year before hanging up his gloves for good.

On 11 April 1995 Zeljko Mavrovic stepped into the ring to face Frenchman Christophe Bizot for the vacant European heavyweight championship. The contest took place in France and was all over in round eleven with Mavrovic winning by a stoppage. As a result, Mavrovic became the first boxer from Croatia to claim this title.

George Foreman retained his IBF world heavyweight title on 22 April 1995, outpointing German challenger Axel Schulz over twelve rounds in Las Vegas (previously, Foreman had been stripped of the WBA version of the championship due to his failure to meet the WBA's number one contender, Tony Tucker).

Since the contest was also for the vacant WBU crown, Foreman became that organization's first holder of the championship in this weight division.

Axel Schulz, who had failed to win the IBF world crown from George Foreman in 1995, was born on 9 November 1968 – the same year that Foreman won the heavy-weight gold medal at the Olympic Games in Mexico.

When George Foreman defeated Axel Schulz in 1995, he became the oldest man to defend a version of the world heavyweight championship. Having been born on 10 January 1949, Foreman was aged forty-six years, three months and twelve days.

Frank Bruno made his first professional boxing appearance in Scotland on 13 May 1995, knocking out American Mike Evans in the second of a ten-round contest which took place in Glasgow.

Jorge Luis Gonzalez became the first Cuban boxer to challenge for a version of the world heavyweight championship on 17 June 1995. Any expectations of victory were dashed in the sixth round in Las Vegas when defending WBO title-holder Riddick Bowe retained his crown by a knockout.

On 19 August 1995 Joe Hipp attempted to become the first Native American to hold a version of the world heavyweight title when he challenged WBA title-holder Bruce Seldon in Las Vegas.

However, it was obvious that Seldon had no intention of smoking the peace pipe when he duly stopped Hipp, a member of the Blackfoot tribe, in round ten.

Credit where credit is due ... just when it looked as if Frank Bruno's dream of one day becoming a world heavyweight champion looked like remaining just that – a dream – a fourth opportunity came his way. On 2 September 1995 WBC title-holder Oliver McCall was tempted to defend against the former European title-holder at Wembley. After twelve absorbing rounds, the championship changed hands when Bruno was declared the winner on points. Thus, McCall became the first American to win the world title from one Briton (Lennox Lewis) and lose it to another Briton (Bruno).

In October 1995 Scott Welch defeated title-holder James Oyebola to become the first white boxer to hold the British heavyweight crown for ten years

When Frank Bruno took the WBC world heavyweight crown from Oliver McCall in 1995, he created a record, being the first former ABA heavyweight title-holder to win a version of the championship.

Frank had won his ABA title in 1980.

On 27 October 1995, Scott Welch defeated James Oyebola, who was defending his British heavyweight crown and also contesting the vacant Commonwealth and WBO Inter-continental heavyweight titles. The championship took place in Brighton, East Sussex, and was stopped in round ten.

His victory made Welch the first white boxer to hold the British heavyweight title since Welshman David Pearce, who reigned from 1983–5.

Earnie Shavers was considered by many to be the hardest puncher in his era. During a long and successful career Shavers had taken part in eighty-nine professional bouts, winning seventy-four (sixty-eight inside the distance), losing fourteen and drawing just one. But on 24 November 1995, Shavers had his last contest when Brian Yates knocked him out in round two in Wisconsin.

Shavers had challenged twice for the world crown. On his first attempt, which took place in New York on 29 September 1977 he lost a fifteen-round points decision to Muhammad Ali. A second attempt, in Las Vegas against the then WBC world heavyweight king Larry Holmes on 28 September 1979, also ended in failure when the contest was stopped in round eleven.

Despite his failure to win a world title, there was no doubting that Shavers was a dangerous man in the ring. With his power, more often than not, if he found his opponent's chin, it was 'goodnight from them'.

On 9 December 1995 Frans Botha of South Africa met Germany's Axel Schulz to contest the vacant IBF world heavyweight title, which had been relinquished by America's George Foreman.

The bout, which was held in Stuttgart, Germany, went the full twelve rounds, with Botha being given the decision on points. However, Botha's joy was later replaced with dismay when he failed a post-fight drugs test and was stripped of the championship. The bout was declared a 'no contest'.

Frans Botha won the vacant IBF world heavyweight crown in December 1995, but was later stripped of the title when he failed a drugs test

Frank Bruno lost his WBC heavyweight title in his first defence to former champion Mike Tyson on 16 March 1996 in Las Vegas, having been stopped in the third round. This proved to be Frank's last professional fight.

During his career in the paid ranks Bruno had forty-five bouts, winning forty and losing five while meeting opponents like Mike Tyson (twice), Lennox Lewis, Oliver McCall, James Smith, Tim Witherspoon, Gerrie Coetzee, Joe Bugner, Lucien Rodriguez, and James Tillis.

Strange to say, but while Bruno won both World and European titles, he did not challenge for the British or Commonwealth crowns during his career.

Former WBC world heavyweight champion Lennox Lewis and former WBO king Ray Mercer met in a ten-round contest in New York on 10 May 1996. After a hard-fought contest, Lewis emerged the winner on points.

Both Lewis and Mercer had boxed in the 1988 Olympic Games, which had been staged in South Korea. Mercer won gold in the heavyweight division and Lewis took the gold medal at super-heavyweight.

Henry Akinwande (right) with Jimmy Thunder (left). Akinwande won the vacant Commonwealth heavyweight crown on 18 March 1993 and the vacant European heavyweight title on 1 May 1993

On 29 June 1996 in Indio, California, Britain's Henry Akinwande captured the vacant WBO world heavyweight title when he knocked out American opponent Jeremy Williams in three rounds.

At the listed height of 6 ft 7 in., Akinwande then created a record by becoming the tallest man to hold a version of the world heavyweight title.

When Henry Akinwande won the WBO world heavyweight title in 1996, he became the second former ABA champion to capture a version of the world crown in this division (Frank Bruno having been the first).

Akinwande won the ABA title at heavyweight in 1988 and 1989.

Russia's Nikolay Valuev made his British professional debut on 8 October 1996, stopping Neil Kirkwood in two rounds at Battersea in London.

On 26 November in Bethnal Green, London, that same year he fought Darren Fearn, who retired in the first round of the contest. At the time, the fans were watching a fighter who would eventually win a version of the world heavyweight title.

Les Clark

Henry Akinwande (here with his Commonwealth trophy) went on to capture the vacant WBO world heavyweight crown in June 1996, knocking out opponent Jeremy Williams in round three

On 9 November 1996 Henry Akinwande defended his WBO world heavyweight title in Las Vegas against challenger Alexander Zolkin, who was stopped in round ten. Zolkin was the first Russian boxer to challenge for a version of the world heavyweight championship.

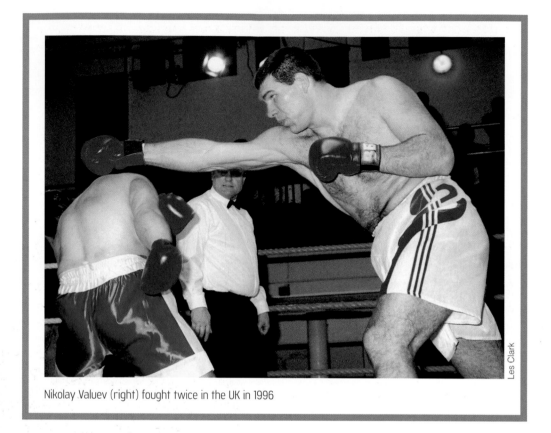

Nikolay Valuev (right) fought twice in the UK in 1996

Few, if any, felt that Evander Holyfield had any chance against the then reigning WBA heavyweight champion Mike Tyson in Las Vegas on 9 November 1996. Tyson had stopped the then holder Bruce Seldon in one round to win the title on 7 September 1996.

However, Holyfield proved to be a revelation, boxing in a commanding way to shock the critics by stopping Tyson in round eleven. The contest was hard fought, with Holyfield becoming only the second man in the history of the sport to regain the title twice (Muhammad Ali being the first).

On 11 January 1997 WBO world heavyweight king Henry Akinwande made the second defence of his title against challenger Scott Welch in Nashville, USA, In a contest that was devoid of excitement. Akinwande retained his crown with a twelve-round points victory.

However, this bout stood out at the time because it was the first time that two British boxers had fought each other for a version of the world heavyweight title on American soil.

Throughout his long and illustrious professional career, former WBC and IBF world heavyweight champion Larry Holmes fought just once in Europe. This occasion took place on 24 January 1997 in Copenhagen when Holmes challenged Denmark's defending title-holder Brian Nielsen for the IBO heavyweight title.

Holmes' bid for the crown ended in failure when losing a twelve-round points decision to the home fighter.

Lennox Lewis became the first British – and, indeed, European – to regain the world heavyweight crown. This occasion took place on 7 February 1997 in Las Vegas when Lewis contested the vacant WBC title (which had been relinquished by Mike Tyson some months after he had taken it from Frank Bruno) against the opponent who defeated him for the championship in 1994, Oliver McCall.

During the course of this contest, McCall appeared to have had a breakdown. Lewis stopped McCall in five rounds.

Lennox Lewis regained his WBC world heavyweight title in February 1997

Pele Reid, then undefeated in seven professional contests (all inside the distance) with five of his victories coming in the first round, was expected to beat opponent Michael Murray on 25 February 1997. It was felt that ring-wise Murray would provide Reid with his sternest fight to date, giving him a few problems to overcome. However, nothing could have been further from the truth, since the quickest ever win in a heavyweight contest (and, for that matter, a British ring) was recorded that night in Sheffield, with the bout being halted in just *nine seconds*. Murray had sustained a dislocated shoulder in the first few seconds of the contest.

On 28 June 1997 Britain's Herbie Hide captured the vacant WBO world heavyweight title (relinquished by Henry Akinwande) when he stopped former IBF king Tony Tucker of America in two rounds in Norwich. In so doing, Hide became the first man to regain this particular version of the championship.

The Hide–Tucker 1997 contest was the first world heavyweight title fight to be staged in Norfolk, England.

The return contest between Evander Holyfield and Mike Tyson for the WBA world heavyweight championship took place in Las Vegas on 28 June 1997. It proved to be an encounter which was astonishing, to say the least. Holyfield retained the crown when Tyson was disqualified in round three after biting both of Holyfield's ears.

On 4 October 1997 Andrew Golota became the first boxer from Poland to contest a version of the world heavyweight championship. However, in Atlantic City, USA,

Les Clark

Don King (centre) with Michael Moorer (left) and Evander Holyfield at a press conference before a championship bout between the two boxers

defending title-holder Lennox Lewis crushed Golota's hopes of victory and glory when he retained his title by a one-round stoppage.

Evander Holyfield, the WBA champion, met the reigning IBF king, Michael Moorer, on 8 November 1997 in Las Vegas in a unification contest. Not only did Holyfield become a dual title-holder when Moorer retired in round eight, but he gained revenge over the southpaw for a previous defeat which had taken place in April 1994 when Moorer had outpointed Holyfield over twelve rounds to win the WBA and IBF world crowns in Las Vegas.

143

In the world amateur boxing championships held in Hungary in 1997, Cuban heavyweight Felix Savon created a record by winning an amazing sixth consecutive gold medal.

Previous gold medals by Savon had been won at the following championships:

★ Reno, USA (1986)
★ Moscow, USSR (1989)
★ Sydney, Australia (1991)
★ Tampere, Finland (1993)
★ Berlin, Germany (1995)

Certainly, Felix was as happy as a cat with all the cream when it came to the heavyweight amateurs.

In 1997 Blue Stevens won the ABA heavyweight title. In so doing, he emulated his father, Les Stevens, who had won the crown in 1971.

On 18 April 1998 Herbie Hide made a successful defence of his WBO world heavyweight crown by stopping American challenger Damon Reed in the first round. Thus, a new record was created for the quickest win in a world heavyweight championship contest: the bout lasted only *fifty-two seconds*!

The 1998 Hide–Reed encounter was the first world heavyweight title contest to take place in Manchester, England.

On 26 September 1998 Zeljko Mavrovic failed in his attempt to win the WBC world heavyweight title when outpointed over twelve rounds by Britain's defending champion Lennox Lewis in Uncasville, USA. However, Mavrovic, with his trademark Mohawk-style haircut, can lay claim to being the first boxer from Croatia to challenge for the heavyweight crown.

Vitali Klitschko put Ukraine on the international boxing map when he became the first boxer from that country to win the European heavyweight crown. Klitschko achieved this feat on 24 October 1998 in Hamburg, when he stopped Germany's Mario Schiesser in round two to capture the vacant championship.

Vitali Klitschko was the first boxer from Ukraine to win the European heavyweight title

Les Clark

As in life, as in boxing – often the first time you know of a disaster is when it hits you. On 5 December 1998 Wladimir Klitschko, Vitah's brother, stepped into the ring in Kiev to face American opponent Ross Puritty in defence of his WBC International heavyweight title.

In truth, it looked like a routine night's work for the Ukrainian boxer. Klitschko was a man who looked to be headed for the top with an undefeated record of twenty-four bouts to his credit. Puritty was an experienced boxer who knew his way around the ring, but it was felt that Klitschko would continue his winning run on the way to a future world heavyweight title challenge. That assessment proved incorrect when Puritty emerged the victor by way of a stoppage in round eleven.

On 13 March 1999, WBC title-holder Lennox Lewis and WBA and IBF king Evander Holyfield met in New York for a contest that was an attempt to unify the three titles. After twelve rounds most observers felt that Lewis had done enough to win. However, the judges considered the contest a draw. There was much argument and debate in the weeks to follow, but the result held. The only remedy would be for the two fighters to meet in the ring a second time.

On 3 April 1999 Julius Francis retained his British and Commonwealth heavyweight titles when he outpointed challenger Danny Williams over twelve rounds in Kensington, London. Thus, Francis became the last man at the weight to win a Lonsdale belt outright by gaining three British championship victories.

A rule was later introduced whereby a boxer had to win four title fights before he could call the belt his own property.

Vitali Klitschko won the WBO version of the world heavyweight title on 26 June 1999 when he knocked out defending champion Herbie Hide in two rounds at Millwall in London. Thus, Klitschko became the first boxer from Ukraine to win a version of the title.

Also, at the listed height of 6 ft 7 in., Klitschko became the joint tallest man (with Britain's Henry Akinwande) at that time in the history of the sport to wear the crown.

Les Clark

Julius Francis (right) retained his British and Commonwealth heavyweight titles with a twelve-round points decision over Danny Williams (left) in April 1999

Wladimir Klitschko won the vacant European heavyweight title on 25 September 1999 in Köln, Germany, when he stopped his German opponent, Axel Schulz, in the eighth round.

It looked like a case of 'keeping it in the family' since the Ukrainian had captured the title which his older brother Vitali had relinquished. This was an historic occasion as it was the first time two brothers had held this crown in succession.

In addition, on defeating Schulz, Klitschko also retained his WBA Inter-Continental heavyweight crown.

Cuban Jose Ribalta bid farewell to the active rigours of professional boxing on 8 October 1999 when he was stopped in the first round by Donovan 'Razor' Ruddock of Canada in a contest that took place in New York.

During a successful career Jose did not challenge for the heavyweight title. However, he met a host of fighters who had at one time held, or who went on to claim, a major version of the championship: James Smith, Mike Tyson, Leon Spinks, Tim Witherspoon, Bruce Seldon, Frank Bruno, Mike Dokes, Larry Holmes, Tony Tubbs, Vitali Klitschko, and Chris Byrd – a most impressive list of top notch-fighters!

Lennox Lewis became the first British boxer in a century to unify the world heavyweight titles

Les Clark

On 13 November 1999 Lennox Lewis made history when he became the first British boxer in a century to unify the world heavyweight titles. In front of a good-natured crowd in Las Vegas, Lewis put his WBC crown on the line against Evander Holyfield's WBA and IBF versions of the title plus the vacant IBO championship.

After twelve robust rounds of boxing, the arm of Lewis was lifted in victory when he was given the decision on points.

CHAPTER EIGHT

HEAVYWEIGHT BOXING IN THE TWENTY-FIRST CENTURY

Former world heavyweight king Mike Tyson made his professional debut in Britain on 29 January 2000 against the then British heavyweight champion Julius Francis.

The bout, staged in Manchester, saw the American stop his British opponent in two explosive rounds. It was clear from the start that Mike did not intend to spend all night in the ring. Francis was brave under fire and attempted to fight back, but Tyson's power was just too much for him.

On paper it looked like a safe defence for defending title-holder, Julius Francis, who was up against Mike Holden for the British championship.

Holden had a record of just eleven bouts, winning seven and losing four. When it was also taken into consideration that Francis had previously outpointed Holden over ten rounds on 9 July 1996, it was clear who the winner was going to be – or was it?

On the night of 13 March 2000 at Bethnal Green in London, Holden provided a shock and won a twelve-round points decision, to be crowned the new British heavyweight champion.

149

Julius Francis was stopped in two rounds by Mike Tyson in January 2000

Les Clark

American Chris Byrd became just the second boxer in the history of the sport with a southpaw stance to win a version of the world heavyweight title. Byrd achieved this feat on 1 April 2000 in Berlin, Germany, when defending WBO king Vitali Klitschko retired on his stool in round nine due to a reported rotary cuff injury.

Lennox Lewis retained his WBC, IBF and IBO versions of the world heavyweight championship with ultimate ease when knocking out American challenger Michael Grant in two rounds in 29 April 2000.

The bout staged in New York became the heaviest world heavyweight title contest in the history of the sport at that time. Lewis hit the scales at a reported 17 st 9 lb and Grant came in at 17 st 12 lb.

Prior to meeting Grant, Lewis had relinquished the WBA portion of the championship rather than fight their nominated challenger John Ruiz.

Les Clark

Chris Byrd became just the second boxer with the southpaw stance to capture the WBO heavyweight crown when in April 2000 he stopped holder Vitali Klitschko, who retired in round nine

Freeda George Foreman made her professional debut on 18 June 2000, knocking out her opponent, Laquanda Landers, in round two in Las Vegas. Her father is a

former two-time, world heavyweight champion. No prizes for guessing who he is, since the clue is clearly in the name – yes, George Foreman is the man!

On 18 June 2000 Maria Johansson made her professional debut in Las Vegas against opponent Karrie Frye, losing on points over four rounds. Maria's father is former world and European heavyweight champion Ingemar Johansson.

Future world heavyweight champion Wladimir Klitschko made his British debut on 15 July 2000 at Millwall in London against opponent Monte Barrett. The fight was all over in round seven with the American proving to be no match for the skills of Klitschko.

Evander Holyfield won the vacant WBA world heavyweight title on 12 August 2000 when he outpointed John Ruiz over twelve rounds in Las Vegas. The WBA version of the crown had been relinquished by Lennox Lewis. Thus, Holyfield thus became the first man in the division to regain the world title for the third time.

The Holyfield–Ruiz contest marked the first occasion for different coloured gloves to be used in a world heavyweight title bout. Holyfield's gloves were white and purple; Ruiz wore gloves coloured black and white.

Chris Byrd of the USA became the first boxer to win the world heavyweight title from one man, only to lose in his first defence to the brother of the fighter he had won the championship from. This event took place on 14 October 2000 in Köln, Germany, when Ukrainian Wladimir Klitschko (brother of Vitali) outpointed Byrd over twelve rounds to take the WBO crown, and thus avenge his brother's defeat.

It would have been a fitting end for a Hollywood film when Danny Williams defended his Commonwealth and WBO Inter-Continental titles, and thus won the vacant British heavyweight championship at Wembley on 21 October 2000.

During this exciting contest against Mark Potter, Williams dislocated his shoulder in round three, but revealed a real fighting heart by fighting through the pain to stop his opponent in round six.

In the 2000 Olympic Games, held in Sydney, Australia, Briton Audley Harrison won a gold medal in the Super-heavyweight division. In doing so, Harrison became the first man ever to win this title for Great Britain.

Previously British-born Lennox Lewis had won this title at the 1988 Olympic Games, but was at the time representing his adopted country of Canada.

Felix Savon of Cuba emulated his fellow countryman Téofilo Stevenson at the 2000 Olympic Games in Sydney, Australia, when he became just the

Audley Harrison won a gold medal at super-heavyweight at the 2000 Olympic Games, but failed to live up to his early promise when he turned professional

Les Clark

Henry Cooper was inducted into the International Boxing Hall of Fame and, in 2000, became the first boxer to receive a knighthood

second man in the history of the sport to win three successive gold medals at heavyweight.

Previously, Savon had won gold medals at the following games:

★ Barcelona, Spain (1992)
★ Atlanta, USA (1996)

Henry Cooper made history in the year 2000 when he became the first boxer to be knighted. Thus 'our 'enry' became *Sir* Henry. During his professional career Cooper fought fifty-five bouts, winning forty, drawing one and losing just fourteen.

On 3 March 2001 John Ruiz punched his way to a twelve-round points decision to take the WBA world heavyweight title from defending champion Evander Holyfield in Las Vegas. In doing so, Ruiz became the first Latino fighter to hold a version of the world heavyweight crown.

On 22 April 2001 in South Africa American Hasim Rahman shocked the experts when he knocked out Britain's Lennox Lewis in five rounds to capture the WBC,

IBF and IBO versions of the world heavyweight title. On that occasion referee Daniel Van de Wiele became the first man from Belgium to referee a world heavyweight championship contest.

The much touted Audley Harrison made his professional debut on 19 May 2001 at Wembley against American Michael Middleton. The Super-heavyweight gold medallist from the 2000 Sydney Olympic Games made short work of his opponent, stopping him in the first round.

Perhaps it would have been a little sarcastic to have asked Danny Williams what took him so long. On 9 June 2001 Williams defended his Commonwealth heavyweight title against New Zealand challenger Kali Meehan at Bethnal

Les Clark

In March 2001 John Ruiz became the first Latino fighter to win a world heavyweight crown, outpointing defending WBA title-holder Evander Holyfield over twelve rounds

Green in London. Williams really went to work early and produced some heavy hitting, which resulted in him retaining his crown in fine style by a stoppage in the first round. The win by Williams took just thirty-two seconds, thus, at the time, setting a new record by being the quickest ever victory in a Commonwealth heavyweight championship bout.

Eddie Futch was in the opposite corner on three occasions when Muhammad Ali was defeated

Les Clark

American Eddie Futch passed away at the age of ninety on 10 October 2001, having been born on 9 August 1911.

Eddie had contributed a great deal to the sport during his many years as a boxer, trainer and corner man. Muhammad Ali must have had nightmares when he knew that Futch would be working in the opposite corner while he was in the ring. Since three of Eddie's fighters – Joe Frazier, Ken Norton and Larry Holmes – all defeated Ali in the professional ranks, this one fact alone must secure Eddie's legacy in the heavyweight division.

On 12 October 2001 Donovan 'Razor' Ruddock regained the vacant Canadian heavyweight championship when he stopped Egerton Marcus in round ten. This was the first Canadian title fight to take place on the *American* side of Niagara Falls.

In Las Vegas on 17 November 2001, Lennox Lewis produced his best to show that he was still the main man in the division when he knocked out American title-holder Hasim Rahman in four rounds to regain the WBC, IBF and IBO versions of the world heavyweight titles.

Lewis now became the first British and, indeed, European heavyweight to regain the championship twice.

On 15 December 2001 Evander Holyfield challenged John Ruiz for the WBA world heavyweight crown in Mashantucket, Connecticut, and came close to regaining the title for an incredible fourth time. When the result was given, a draw over twelve rounds was declared.

When Evander Holyfield was given a draw in his world title bid against John Ruiz in 2001, he became the first man to be given a drawn result in *two* world heavyweight title bouts. The first had taken place on 13 March 1999 in a unification contest against Lennox Lewis.

Donovan 'Razor' Ruddock won the vacant Canadian heavyweight crown in the first Canadian heavyweight bout to be staged on the American side of the Niagara Falls in October 2001

In the 2001 world amateur world championships, which took place in Belfast, Northern Ireland, David Haye came so very close to becoming England's first champion at heavyweight when he faced Cuban Odlanier Fonte Solis in the final.

Haye made a good start, but was stopped in the third round by Solis and had to settle for the silver medal. However, this was no small achievement considering the class opposition taking part in the championships.

It was a contest long overdue between two fighting men who had to meet to see who was the best. On 8 June 2002 in Memphis, Tennessee, Lennox Lewis retained his WBC, IBF and IBO heavyweight titles by knocking out the once most feared fighter on the planet – Mike Tyson – in round eight. While Lewis fought a good fight and was punch-perfect in every way, it was clear that this was not the Tyson of old; Tyson was exchanging punches, but that trademark burning desire of his was no longer apparent.

However, this should not take the shine off a fine victory for the British fighter who, at that moment in time, had cleared up all opposition at the weight and looked well on his way to being ranked with the true greats in the division.

Give that woman a bouquet of flowers – Diane Lee Fischer furthered the cause of women in boxing when she became the first female to promote a world heavyweight title fight. The fight took place in Atlantic City, USA, on 29 June 2002 when defending WBO champion Wladimir Klitschko of Ukraine stopped former champion Ray Mercer of the USA in the sixth round.

Przemyslaw Saleta became Poland's first European heavyweight champion on 20 July 2002 when he stopped Germany's defending title-holder Luan Krasniqi in round nine. The contest took place in Dortmund, Germany.

In Las Vegas on 27 July 2002, John Ruiz retained his WBA world heavyweight title by way of a ten-round disqualification against Canadian challenger Kirk Johnson. This was the fifth heavyweight title bout since the introduction of the Marquess of Queensberry Rules to end in a disqualification.

DISQUALIFICATION

BOXERS	RESULT	DATE
Max Schmeling — vs — Jack Sharkey	Schmeling won vacant title in round 4	12 Jun 1930
Joe Louis — vs — Buddy Baer	Louis retained title in round 7	23 May 1941
Evander Holyfield — vs — Mike Tyson	Holyfield retained WBA title in round 3	28 Jun 1997
Lennox Lewis — vs — Henry Akinwande	Lewis retained WBC title in round 5	12 Jul 1997

Some records show that the 1982 Holmes–Cooney WBC contest, in which Holmes retained his title in round thirteen, ended in a disqualification victory for the champion. However, it is now generally acknowledged that this was a thirteen-round stoppage win for Holmes.

On 17 August 2002 Laila Ali won the IBA super-middleweight crown when she stopped Suzetta Taylor in two rounds in Las Vegas. In so doing, Laila became the first daughter of a former world heavyweight champion to win a world boxing title. Who was her father? None other than the great man himself, Muhammad Ali, who was actually ringside to see Laila win the championship.

Les Clark

Laila Ali won the IBA version of the world super-middleweight title in August 2002, stopping opponent Suzetta Taylor in two rounds

In defence of his British and Commonwealth heavyweight titles, Danny Williams outpointed challenger Keith Long over twelve rounds at Bethnal Green in London on 17 September 2002. Thus, Danny became the first British champion in the division to win the belt outright by having to gain four title victories. (To gain ownership of said belt one of the defences must be mandatory.) Previously, a fighter kept the much-sought after belt after only three championship victories.

Sinan Samil Sam put his name into the record books on 12 October 2002 when he captured the European heavyweight crown in Schwerin, Germany, by stopping defending champion Przemyslaw Saleta of Poland in round seven. Samil Sam thus became the first Turkish boxer to win this title.

British and Commonwealth heavyweight champion Danny Williams looked as if he had a good chance of being the first British holder of the European title since Henry Akinwande who reigned from 1993–5. However, Danny failed in his bid on 8 February 2003 when defending title-holder Sinan Samil Sam stopped him in round six in Berlin, Germany.

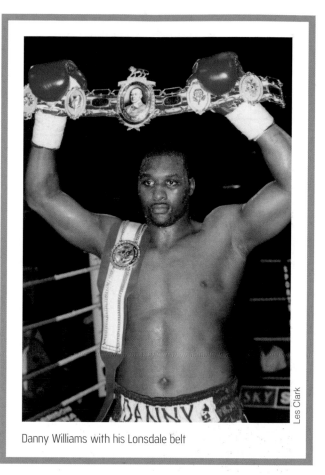

Danny Williams with his Lonsdale belt

On 1 March 2003 a man by the name of Roy Jones, Jnr, produced a little ring magic by defeating holder John Ruiz by way of a twelve-round points decision for the WBA world heavyweight title in Las Vegas. Jones created a new chapter to the history of boxing by becoming the first former world middleweight champion (IBF version) since Bob Fitzsimmons, who had reigned in the division from 1891–3, to win a version of the world heavyweight crown. For the record, Jones was also a former IBF world super-middleweight and undisputed light-heavyweight champion.

Many fight fans must have been filled with shock when, on 8 March 2003, South African Corrie Sanders demolished defending WBO heavyweight king Wladimir Klitschko of Ukraine in two rounds in Hanover, Germany.

At the time Klitschko was not only the favourite to retain his crown but a fighter who many experts felt would go on to be a major force in the division. Sanders became just the third boxer with a southpaw stance to hold a version of the championship.

Cory Spinks won the IBF version of the world welterweight title in Italy when he outpointed Italian holder Michele Piccirillo over twelve rounds on 22 March 2003.

While he may have been boxing in a lighter division, Cory is strongly connected to the heavyweight division in no uncertain way: his father, Leon Spinks, is a former undisputed world heavyweight champion and his uncle, Michael Spinks, is a former holder of the IBF world heavyweight crown as well as being a former undisputed world light-heavyweight champion.

Lennox Lewis retained his WBC and IBO versions of the world heavyweight title on 21 June 2003 in a hard-fought contest, stopping former European and WBO king Vitali Klitschko in round six.

The bout took place in Los Angeles – the first heavyweight championship to be staged there since August 1958 when the then defending champion Floyd Patterson stopped challenger Roy Harris in round twelve.

The Lewis–Klitschko world title bout found a place in the boxing history books by being the heaviest heavyweight title bout to date. Lewis came in at a reported 18 st 4 lb and Klitschko at 17 st 10 lb. The fighters in the division appeared to be getting larger and larger. A great deal of poundage stood in the ring on the night.

Some months after defeating Vitali Klitschko, Lennox Lewis decided to call it a day in 2004 and thus retired from the sport he had served so well after winning the World, British, European and Commonwealth heavyweight titles.

Lewis had a fine professional record of forty-four bouts, winning forty-one, losing just two and drawing only one of his bouts. Lennox also gained revenge over the two men who had managed to defeat him: Oliver McCall and Hasim Rahman. The draw against Evander Holyfield was also avenged when the pair met again. There can be no doubt that Lennox Lewis deserves to be ranked with the greats of the division.

During his professional career Lennox Lewis met more boxers who had already won, or who would go on to win, the world heavyweight title than any other British boxer. The boxers in question were: Mike Weaver, Tony Tucker, Frank Bruno, Oliver McCall, Tommy Morrison, Ray Mercer, Henry Akinwande, Shannon Briggs, Evander Holyfield, Hasim Rahman, Mike Tyson, and Vitali Klitschko. (Frans Botha is omitted because his winning bout was declared a 'no contest'.)

Matt Skelton won the vacant WBU title in February 2005, stopping opponent Fabio Eduardo Moli in six rounds

When Lennox Lewis retired he held the record of having taken part in more world heavyweight title bouts (18) than any other British fighter at the weight to date.

EIGHTEEN CHAMPIONSHIP HEAVYWEIGHT BOUTS FOR

OPPONENT	RESULTS FOR LEWIS	DATE
Tony Tucker	won: twelve-round points decision .... (first defence) (WBC version of title)	8 May 1993
Frank Bruno	won: referee stopped contest in round seven .... (WBC version of title)	1 Oct 1993
Phil Jackson	won: referee stopped contest in round eight.... (WBC version of title)	6 May 1994
Oliver McCall	lost: referee stopped contest in round two...... (WBC version of title)	24 Sep 1994
Oliver McCall	won: referee stopped contest in round five ...... (regained vacant WBC version of title)	7 Feb 1997
Henry Akinwande	won: by disqualification in round five .... (WBC version of title)	12 Jul 1997
Andrew Golota	won: referee stopped contest in round one ...... (WBC version of title)	4 Oct 1997
Shannon Briggs	won: referee stopped contest in round five .... (WBC version of title)	28 Mar 1998
Zeljko Mavrovic	won: twelve-round points decision .... (WBC version of title)	26 Sep 1998

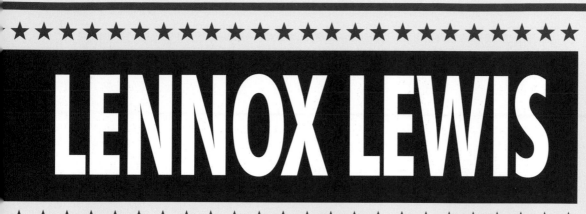

LENNOX LEWIS

OPPONENT	RESULTS FOR LEWIS	DATE
Evander Holyfield	**drew: over twelve rounds** .... (Lewis's WBC and Holyfield's WBA and IBF versions of the title were at stake)	13 Mar 1999
Evander Holyfield	**won: twelve-round points decision**.............. (Lewis's WBC and Holyfield's WBA and IBF versions of the title were at stake – also the vacant IBO title)	13 Nov 1999
Michael Grant	**won: by a knockout in round two** .... (WBC, IBF and IBO versions of the title)	29 Apr 2000
Frans Botha	**won: referee stopped contest in round two** ..... (WBC, IBF and IBO versions of the title)	15 Jul 2000
David Tua	**won: twelve-round points decision**............. (WBC, IBF and IBO versions of the title)	11 Nov 2000
Hasim Rahman	**lost: by a knockout in round five** .... (WBC, IBF and IBO versions of the title)	22 Apr 2001
Hasim Rahman	**won: by a knockout in round four**.............. (regained WBC, IBF and IBO versions of the title)	17 Nov 2001
Mike Tyson	**won: by a knockout in round eight** .... (WBC, IBF and IBO versions of the title)	8 Jun 2002
Vitali Klitschko	**won: referee stopped contest in round six** ..... (WBC and IBO versions of the title)	21 Jun 2003

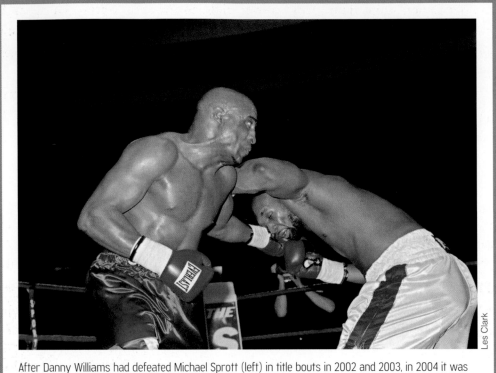

Les Clark

After Danny Williams had defeated Michael Sprott (left) in title bouts in 2002 and 2003, in 2004 it was third time lucky for Sprott, who outpointed title-holder Danny Williams over twelve rounds to capture the British & Commonwealth heavyweight titles

Matt Skelton became the first holder of the English heavyweight title when he faced former British heavyweight champion Mike Holden in the inaugural contest, which took place on 18 September 2003 in Dagenham, Essex. Hard-punching Matt stopped his man in the sixth round to win the newly created belt.

The old saying 'third time lucky' proved right for Michael Sprott when, on 24 January 2004, at the third time of asking, he outpointed holder Danny Williams over twelve rounds to capture the British and Commonwealth heavyweight titles at Wembley.

Sprott's two previous challenges to Williams had ended in failure, having retired in round seven on 12 February 2002 and having been stopped in round five on 26 September 2003.

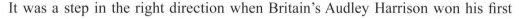

It was a step in the right direction when Britain's Audley Harrison won his first professional title (WBF heavyweight) on 20 March 2004 by knocking out holder Richel Hersisia in four rounds at Wembley. At this stage of his career, southpaw Harrison was now undefeated in fifteen bouts.

In an unexpected turn of events Wladimir Klitschko failed to regain the WBO version of the world heavyweight title when American Lamon Brewster stopped him for the vacant crown in round five on 10 April 2004 in Las Vegas.

True, it may not have been a contest of epic proportions when John Ruiz retained his WBA world heavyweight

Les Clark

Hard-punching Lamon Brewster retained his WBO world heavyweight crown against challenger Luan Krasniqi

title belt against challenger Fres Oquendo. Ruiz won by way of a stoppage in round eleven. However, the contest, which was fought in New York on 17 April 2004, finds itself in the record books by virtue of it being the first time that two Latinos had contested a world heavyweight championship.

Matt Skelton punched his way to the British and Commonwealth heavyweight titles on 24 April 2004 in Reading, England, by knocking out defending champion Michael Sprott in round twelve. Thus, Skelton secured for himself a place in the history books for he won the championship in the quickest period of time, having had his first professional contest on 22 September 2002.

Following the retirement of Lennox Lewis, Vitali Klitschko of Ukraine won the vacant WBC world heavyweight title on 24 April 2004 in Los Angeles by a stoppage in the eighth round. This win restored pride to the Klitschko family since the man Vitali defeated was South African Corrie Sanders, the man who had torn the WBO heavyweight crown from his younger brother Wladimir in two rounds in 2003.

Who knows? Perhaps every time Vitali threw a telling punch he may have been thinking 'that's for my little brother!'

It looked as if a fly in a spider's web had more chance of survival than former British and Commonwealth heavyweight champion Danny Williams when matched with former world heavyweight king Mike Tyson in Louisville, Kentucky, on 30 July 2004. Tyson may have been past his best, but he was still a formidable force in the division. However, upsets do happen and Danny provided one of the major shocks of the year when he knocked out the American in round four to record his best victory to date.

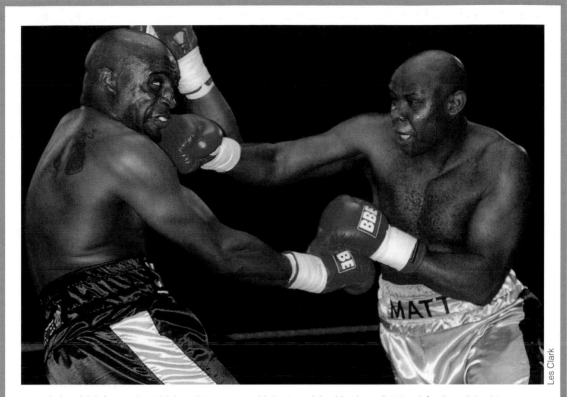

Matt Skelton (right) won the British and Commonwealth heavyweight titles in April 2004, defeating Michael Sprott

Jacqui Frazier-Lyde won the UBA world women's heavyweight title on 10 September 2004 against fellow American Mary Ann Almager, whom she outpointed over ten rounds in Atlantic City, USA. Jacqui's father is former world heavyweight champion of the world Joe Frazier.

On 13 November 2004 Chris Byrd retained his IBF world heavyweight crown when he outpointed Jameel McCline over twelve rounds in New York. Challenger McCline may have lost the contest but he edged his way into the record books when, at the reported weight of 19 st 4 lb, he became the joint heaviest man along with Primo Carnera to contest a world heavyweight title.

Danny Williams experienced the 'one day you're up' feeling after defeating Mike Tyson in July 2004 and then the 'next day you're down' feeling, when he failed to bring the world heavyweight title back to Britain later the same year.

On 11 December that year, Williams was stopped in round eight by defending WBC title-holder Vitali Klitschko in Las Vegas. This contest made the record books since it became the heaviest championship bout in the history of the sport to date. Klitschko came in at a reported 17 st 12 lb and Williams tipped the scales at 19 st 4 lb. For the record, Williams became the joint heaviest man with Primo Carnera and Jameel McCline, who were the same weight when they fought for the world heavyweight championship.

Former world heavyweight champion Max Schmeling, who must be the greatest heavyweight to be produced in Germany, died on 2 February 2005, aged 99. Max achieved a great deal during his career, winning the European and German heavyweight titles plus the European light-heavyweight crown. However, he will always be remembered as the first man to defeat the great Joe Louis in the professional ranks while Louis was in his prime. Max was born on 28 September 1905.

In his quest for higher honours on the international front, British and Commonwealth heavyweight king Matt Skelton stretched his undefeated professional record to sixteen wins when he defeated Argentina's Fabio Eduardo Moli in six rounds at Wembley on 25 February 2005. Skelton defeated the Argentinian to win his fourth championship belt and capture the vacant WBU heavyweight title.

It really looked as if American James Toney had put his name into the history books of boxing when he became just the third holder of the world middleweight title to win a version of the world heavyweight crown. This event took place at the Madison Square Garden in New York on 30 April 2005.

As not only a former IBF middle, but also super-middle and cruiserweight world title-holder, Toney outpointed WBA holder John Ruiz over twelve rounds. It appeared that Ruiz had become the first holder of a world heavyweight title to twice lose his crown to a former holder of the world middleweight title (the first time being, of course, to Roy Jones Jr in 2003).

The future looked great for Toney, with the prospect of some very lucrative fights on the horizon. However, the situation changed in the weeks that followed when Toney tested positive for a banned substance and was stripped of the title. Hence, the result was changed to a 'no decision' with Ruiz reinstated as champion.

On 21 May 2005 Lamon Brewster retained his WBO world heavyweight title by stopping Poland's Andrew Golota in just fifty-three seconds of the first round in Chicago. The bout proved to be the *second* quickest win in the history of the division. (The fastest title victory was the defence by Britain's Herbie Hide on 18 April 1998 against American Damon Reed in Manchester. Hide retained the championship in just fifty-two seconds.)

It would be very true to say that only very close friends and members of his family gave Kevin McBride from Ireland any sort of chance against former world heavyweight champion Mike Tyson – and even they may have had their doubts. However, on 11 June 2005 McBride proved all the doubters wrong when he created an upset in Washington, DC, by forcing the once indestructible Tyson to retire on his stool at the end of the sixth round.

Every dog has its day – and some days it is the underdog who gets to be top dog.

During their respective professional careers Lennox Lewis and Mike Tyson attained the status of undisputed champion. However, neither boxer held the WBO version of the world heavyweight title during their duration in the ring.

Matt Skelton retained his British heavyweight title in Bolton, Lancashire, on 16 July 2005 when challenger Mark Krence retired in round seven. This contest proved to be significant since it was the last British heavyweight championship to see a referee (Terry O'Connor) being the sole arbitrator. Under new rules for future matches, three judges would render the decision should the bout go the scheduled distance.

Les Clark

Kevin McBride provided an upset in June 2005 when he forced former world heavyweight champion Mike Tyson to retire at the end of round six

Germany's former world heavyweight champion Max Schmeling, who died on 2 February 2005, would have been 100 years of age on 28 September 2005. So one really had to ask if it was an omen that Germany's Luan Krasniqi was challenging WBO heavyweight champion Lamon Brewster of the USA in Hamburg for the title on this date. Had it been an Hollywood movie Krasniqi would have punched his way to the title and glory with the fans on their feet cheering him on to victory. However, this was real life and after a good start Krasniqi retired in round nine after giving his all against the hard-punching Brewster. On this night there would be no celebrations for German boxing fans.

Owing to an injured knee, Vitali Klitschko announced his retirement from the sport in November 2005. In so doing Vitali became the second successive holder of the WBC world heavyweight crown to retire while still holding the crown as Lennox Lewis had done previously. Departing from the sport in 2004, Klitschko left the sport at that time with a professional record of thirty-seven fights, winning thirty-five and losing just two. Both defeats were in world title bouts against Chris Byrd (WBO) and Lennox Lewis (WBC and IBO). The big question now was whether Klitshchko would stay retired or return at a later date.

Following the retirement of Vitali Klitschko, former WBC heavyweight title-holder Hasim Rahman of the USA found himself back on top of the hill once again, when the WBC awarded him the championship. Rahman's success was based on his twelve-round points victory, which had taken place over Monte Barrett in Chicago on 13 August 2005 for the vacant interim title.

The first British heavyweight title bout to have three judges scoring the contest rather than the referee took place on 10 December 2005 at the ExCel Area in London.

The officials in question were: Ian John-Lewis, Mark Green and Richie Davies. However, the judges were rendered redundant when the defending title-holder Matt Skelton stopped his challenger John McDermott in just seventy-nine seconds of the first round to retain his crown.

The former British and Commonwealth heavyweight king Danny Williams met fellow Briton Audley Harrison on the same bill as the Skelton–McDermott encounter to contest the vacant Commonwealth heavyweight championship.

This contest, which saw Harrison lose the bout (and thus his undefeated record after nineteen victories) when he was outpointed over twelve rounds, was by no means an epic battle. However, it was also the first Commonwealth title bout in this division to have three scoring judges at ringside. The officials at that time were: Mark Green, Phil Edwards and Terry O'Connor.

Mark Green can claim a special honour in being one of the first judges to officiate at both British and Commonwealth heavyweight title fights on the very same night.

Tania Follett made history in 1997 by becoming the first female manager to be licensed by the British Boxing Board of Control

Tania Follett is a lady who is quite used to creating boxing history. Indeed, she became the first female to work in the corner of various boxers and then, in 1997, she became the first female in Britain to be licensed as a manager by The British Boxing Board of Control.

On 16 December 2005 in Bracknell, Berkshire, fighter Matt Paice made his professional debut, outpointing opponent Simon Goodwin over four rounds. Paice's manager was Tania Follet so, as a result of this fight, she became the first female in Britain to manage a heavyweight boxer.

History was made in Berlin on 17 December 2005 when Russia's Nikolay Valuev outpointed defending champion

John Ruiz over twelve rounds to win the WBA world heavyweight title. At the listed height of 7 ft 2 in. and at a weight of 23 st 2 lb, Valuev became at that moment in time the tallest and heaviest man to hold a version of the championship. Truly, Valuev was a giant amongst giants.

The title fight between Nikolay Valuev and John Ruiz became the heaviest world heavyweight title fight to date. Nikolay Valuev weighed in at 23 st 2 lb and John Ruiz at 16 st 13½ lb, which begs the question: did the ring need to be reinforced?

Winning the WBA world heavyweight title in 2005 made Nikolay Valuev the first boxer from Russia to hold a version of this championship.

Britain's Matt Skelton had a bad night on 25 February 2006 when he challenged Danny Williams at the ExCel Arena in London for the Commonwealth heavy-weight championship. Since he failed to regain his former title when outpointed over twelve rounds, he lost his undefeated record, which had stood at eighteen prior to stepping into the ring.

Skelton was also stripped of his British heavyweight crown, which was not at stake on this occasion. However, this action was taken because he lost to a fellow British boxer over the championship distance. Some days it is just not worth getting out of bed.

James Toney attempted to become just the third former holder of the world middle-weight title to win a version of the world heavyweight championship when he challenged WBC king Hasim Rahman in Atlantic City on 18 March 2006. However, at the end of a keenly contested twelve-round bout, the fight was called a draw. Which meant that Toney, also a former holder of both the IBF super-middle and cruiserweight titles, failed for the second time to add his name to an elite list.

The Rahman–Toney contest was only the seventh world heavyweight title bout to result in a drawn verdict under the Marquess of Queensberry Rules.

Les Clark

Siarhei Liakhovich won the WBO world heavyweight crown in April 2006 when he outpointed title-holder Lamon Brewster in what was considered by many to be an upset

'Who is that again?' Boxing fans might well have asked when told that Siarhei Liakhovich had become the new WBO world heavyweight champion. Not exactly a household name, Liakhovich pulled off an upset on 1 April 2006 when he outpointed American holder Lamon Brewster over twelve rounds in Cleveland, Ohio, to capture the title. In so doing, Liakhovich became the first Belarussian to capture the crown in this division.

On 22 April 2006, Chris Byrd of America lost his IBF world heavyweight title to Wladimir Klitschko of Ukraine in Mannheim, Germany, when stopped in round seven.

This must have seemed like a case of déjà vu for Byrd. Previously he

DRAWN VERDICT

BOXERS	NO OF ROUNDS LASTED	DATE
Tommy Burns — vs — Philadelphia Jack O'Brien	20	28 Nov 1906
Jack Johnson — vs — Jim Johnson	10	19 Dec 1913
Michael Dokes — vs — Mike Weaver (WBA)	15	20 May 1983
Lennox Lewis — vs — Evander Holyfield (WBC, WBA, IBF)	12	13 Mar 1999
John Ruiz — vs — Evander Holyfield (WBA)	12	15 Dec 2001
Chris Byrd — vs — Andrew Golota (IBF)	12	17 Apr 2004
James Toney — vs — Hasim Rahman	12	18 Mar 2006

had lost the WBO version of the heavyweight championship to Klitschko on 14 October 2000 when defending the crown against him. On that occasion he had been outpointed over twelve rounds. The vacant IBO heavyweight crown was also at stake during the 2006 contest.

When Wladimar Klitschko of Ukraine won the IBF version of the world heavyweight championship, he became the third boxer from the former Soviet Union to simultaneously hold a world heavyweight title. The other world champions at the time were Nikolay Valuev, the WBA holder from Russia, and Siarhei Liakhovich, the WBO champion from Belarus.

At that particular moment, the only non-European holder was WBC king Hasim Rahman of the USA.

Former world heavyweight champion Floyd Patterson passed away on 11 May 2006.

Floyd was born on 4 January 1935. During his time in the professional ranks Patterson garnered a record of sixty-four bouts, winning fifty-five, losing eight and drawing just one. Patterson fought men like Sonny Liston (twice), Muhammad Ali (twice), Archie Moore, Ingemar Johansson (three times), Joey Maxim, Eddie Machen, George Chuvalo, Henry Cooper, Jerry Quarry (twice), Oscar Bonavenna, and Jimmy Ellis.

Floyd's place in boxing history will always be more than secure, since he was the first man to regain the undisputed world heavyweight title, a record which will always stand.

Scott Gammer captured the vacant British heavyweight championship when he stopped opponent Mark Krence in round nine on 16 June 2006 in Carmarthen,

Scott Gammer (left), seen outpointing Micky Steeds in their 2005 meeting, went on to become the first Welshman since David Pearce to win the British heavyweight title in 2006

West Wales. In so doing, Scott became the first Welsh holder of this title since David Pearce, who had reigned from 1983–5.

Prior to Gammer, only six Welsh boxers had held the British heavyweight title: Jack Petersen, Tommy Farr, Johnny Williams, Joe Erskine, Neville Meade, and David Pearce.

Boxing history was made when Kazakhstan-born Oleg Maskaev became the fourth boxer from the former Soviet Union to hold a version of the world heavyweight title when he stopped defending WBC champion Hasim Rahman in the twelfth round in Las Vegas on 12 August 2006.

The other Eastern Europeans to hold a heavyweight crown were Wladimir Klitschko from Ukraine (IBF and IBO), Siarhei Liakhovich from Belarus (WBO), and Russia's Nikolay Valuev (WBA).

In Phoenix, Arizona, USA, on 4 November 2006, Shannon Briggs became the first American to break the hold of the former Soviet Union quartet's on the world heavyweight title when he stopped Belarus' defending WBO holder Siarhei Liakhovich in round twelve.

On 10 November 2006 Turkey's Sinan Samil Sam retained his WBC International heavyweight crown when he outpointed Australian Bob Mirovic over twelve rounds in Hamburg, Germany.

For the first time the new WBC rule of open scoring was introduced in a heavyweight championship contest. This involved the scores of the judges being announced after the fourth and eighth rounds. In so during both the fans and the fighters knew who was winning at that particular point in the bout.

It was time to break open the vodka in celebration when the first-ever world heavyweight title fight in the history of the sport took place in Russia in 2006.

On 10 December that year defending champion Kazakhstan's WBC champion Oleg Maskaev outpointed challenger Okhello Peter over twelve rounds in Moscow to retain his crown.

In 2006 Okhello Peter became the first boxer from Uganda to challenge for a version of the world heavyweight championship.

On 22 December 2006 a very unusual heavyweight contest took place in Berlin when Holland's Harry Duiven Junior stopped his opponent in two rounds to win his bout.

What's so unusual about that? Well, Harry Duiven's opponent was his father, Harry Duiven Senior!

Another entry into the history books of heavyweight boxing was written on 20 January 2007 when the first-ever world championship in the division took place in Switzerland. WBA title-holder Nikolay Valuev retained his crown in Basel when American challenger Jameel McCline was stopped in the third round due to an injury to his left knee.

The Valuev–McCline contest produced another fact of historical significance when it became the heaviest world heavyweight title bout ever staged at that time. Champion Valuev came in at a reported weight of 23 st ¼ lb, while challenger McCline tipped the scales at 19 st 2¼ lb.

On 10 February 2007 in Cleveland, Ohio, American Vonda Ward ensured her place in the history books of the sport when she became the first woman holder of the WBC world heavyweight championship. Vonda accomplished this feat when she outpointed opponent Martha Salazar over ten rounds to capture the vacant crown.

Following his impressive third-round stoppage victory over former British and Commonwealth heavyweight champion Danny Williams on 9 December 2006, it looked as if Audley Harrison was on his way to some major title fights. However,

Ruslan Chagaev became the first boxer from Uzbekistan to win the world heavyweight crown when he outpointed defending WBA champion champion Nikolay Valuev over twelve rounds in April 2007

Les Clark

at Wembley on 17 February 2007 Michael Sprott, the former British and Commonwealth heavyweight title-holder had other ideas about that! In defence of his European Union title and vacant English heavyweight crown, Sprott stopped Harrison in the third round.

The form book was well and truly upset in Stuttgart, Germany, on 14 April 2007 when challenger Ruslan Chagaev outpointed Russia's defending WBA world heavyweight champion Nikolay Valuev over twelve rounds. In so doing Chagaev became the first boxer from Uzbekistan to win this title and just the fourth boxer with the southpaw stance in the division to claim a version of the crown.

On 2 June 2007 Sultan Ibragimov became the second Russian-born and fifth boxer with the southpaw stance to hold a version of the world heavyweight title when he outpointed defending WBO champion Shannon Briggs of America over twelve rounds in Atlantic City. For the first time two southpaws held a world heavyweight title simultaneously (the other champion being WBA king Ruslan Chagaev).

Former world heavyweight champion Evander Holyfield challenged Russia's Sultan Ibragimov in Moscow on 13 October 2007 for the WBO world heavyweight title, but failed in his bid after being outpointed over twelve rounds. However, while Holyfield was unable to claim a victory, he was able to claim a place in the record books by becoming the first American boxer to contest a world heavyweight championship in Russia.

At forty years of age it could be said that youth was not exactly on the side of Britain's reigning Commonwealth heavyweight king Matt Skelton when he challenged WBA world title-holder Ruslan Chagaev of Uzbekistan for the championship. The contest took place in Dusseldorf, Germany, on 19 January 2008 and, after twelve, hard-fought rounds, Chagaev retained his crown with a points decision. However, Skelton did make it into the record books as being the oldest first-time challenger for the world heavyweight title.

It should also be noted that Skelton became the first British boxer in this division to challenge a defending champion who boxed in the southpaw stance.

On 23 February 2008 Ukrainian Wladimir Klitschko successfully defended his IBF and IBO heavyweight titles against Sultan Ibragimov of Russia by

Philip Sharkey

In 2011 Wladimir Klitschko added the WBO version of the world title to the versions he already held (he had won the IBF and IBO crowns when he defeated Sultan Ibragimov in 2008)

way of a twelve-round points decision at Madison Square Garden, New York. In so doing Klitschko also won the WBO version of the title which Ibragimov was defending. Wladimir also took a step nearer to becoming the undisputed world champion.

This bout was the first unification in the division since the Lewis–Holyfield encounter which took place on 13 November 1999. The Klitschko–Ibragimov contest was also the first unification bout at the weight between two boxers from the former Soviet Union.

Samuel Peter won the world heavyweight championship on 8 March 2008 when he stopped defending title-holder Oleg Maskaev in Cancun in six rounds to win the WBC crown. This was the first world heavyweight title contest to be staged in Mexico.

When Samuel Peter won the WBC world heavyweight title he became the first Nigerian boxer to claim the championship for his country. (Herbie Hide, who won the WBO world heavyweight title on two occasions, was born in Nigeria but represented England when he won the championship.)

On 11 April 2008, Martin Rogan became the first man to win the Prize Fighter heavyweight tournament at Bethnal Green, London. To win the competition Rogan stopped Alex Ibbs in round two in the quarterfinal. Then, in the semi-final, Rogan outpointed opponent Dave Ferguson over three rounds. The final saw him face David Dolan, who Rogan outpointed over three rounds to win.

Philip Sharkey

Martin Rogan was the first man to win the prizefighter heavyweight tournament on 11 April 2008

On 30 August 2008 Nikolay Valuev became the first Russian boxer to regain a version of the world heavyweight title when he outpointed former holder John Ruiz for the vacant WBA crown by way of a twelve-round points decision in Berlin, Germany. (The previous champion, Ruslan Chagaev, had had to relinquish the title due to injury.)

After almost four years out of the ring, Ukrainian Vitali Klitschko returned to boxing on 11 October 2008 in Berlin, Germany, and regained the WBC world heavyweight crown from defending Nigerian champion Samuel Peter, who retired at the end of round eight.

As a result, for the first time in the sport's history two brothers in the heavyweight division held different versions of the championship at the same time, with Vitali's younger brother Wladimir holding the IBF, WBO and IBO titles.

On 15 November 2008, in a bout which was a WBC eliminator for the world crown, Britain's David Haye showed in no uncertain fashion that he was a force to be reckoned with when he stopped former world heavyweight title challenger Monte Barrett from the USA in five rounds in a contest which took place in Greenwich, London.

On 19 December 2008 Matt Skelton captured the vacant European heavyweight title in Milan, Italy, when former holder of the championship Paolo Vidoz retired on his stool at the end of round nine. Skelton became the first British boxer to hold this crown since Henry Akinwande, who had reigned from 1993–5.

David Haye (left) stopped Monte Barrett in a bout on 15 November 2008

Philip Sharkey

Ingemar Johansson, the former world and European heavyweight champion, passed away on 30 January 2009. During his career, Johansson fought men like Floyd Patterson (three times), Eddie Machen, Henry Cooper, Dick Richardson, Brian London, Joe Erskine and Joe Bygraves, and compiled an impressive record of twenty-eight bouts, winning twenty-six of them.

Ingemar was born on 22 September 1932.

In a hard-fought battle, which took place in Birmingham on 28 February 2009, Martin Rogan captured the Commonwealth heavyweight title when he stopped defending champion Matt Skelton in round eleven. In so doing, Rogan became the first Irish boxer since Danny McAlinden (who reigned from 1972–5) to hold this crown. While Skelton was also the European champion, this title was not at stake in this contest but was later declared vacant.

Tim Witherspoon Junior, who boxes at the lightweight poundage, fought a draw over four rounds with opponent Gabriel Morris in Cincinnati, Ohio, on 23 May 2009. Tim is the son of former WBC and WBA world heavyweight champion Tim Witherspoon.

A triumphant David Haye wearing his European cruiserweight title belt

George Foreman, Jnr, made his professional debut on 6 June 2009, in Louisiana, USA, knocking out opponent Clyde Weaver in the first round. George is the son of former two-time world heavyweight king George Foreman.

When Tyson Fury won the English heavyweight title on 11 September 2009 at Brentwood in Essex, outpointing defending champion John McDermott over ten rounds, he became at that time the tallest man to hold the championship at a listed height of 6 ft 9 in.

It really did appear that David Haye had a very high mountain to climb when he challenged WBA world heavyweight champion Nikolay Valuev for his title in Versicherung, Nuremberg, Germany, on 7 November 2009. Valuev was listed at the height of 7 ft 2 in and Haye at 6 ft 3 in. There was also a weight difference, with Valuev coming in at a reported 22 st 6½ lb and Haye 15 st 6¾ lb. However, despite the height and weight difference, Haye punched his way to a twelve-round points decision to take the crown from the defending Russian, and thus became Britain's first champion at the weight since Lennox Lewis and just the second former world cruiserweight title-holder to win the title (the first being Evander Holyfield).

Albert Sosnowski became the second boxer from Poland to win the European heavyweight title, outpointing Paolo Vidoz for the vacant crown in December 2009

Philip Sharkey

On 18 December 2009, Albert Sosnowski displayed impressive boxing skills to become just the second boxer from Poland to win the vacant European heavyweight crown when he outpointed former title-holder Paolo Vidoz of Italy over twelve rounds. The contest took place at Bethnal Green in London

In Florida on 16 February 2010 American Elijah McCall lost his contest when Haitian Dieuly Aristilde knocked him out in round four. After surviving a torrid

189

opening round Aristilde was able to turn the fight around and found the punch which said 'good night' to his opponent. Elijah is the son of former WBC world heavyweight champion Oliver McCall.

Britain's David Haye put on an explosive performance at the MEN Area, in Manchester, to ensure that his first defence of the WBA championship would not be his last when he stopped Hispanic-American John Ruiz a former two-time WBA title-holder in nine rounds on 3 April 2010.

Michael Sprott failed to win the European heavyweight crown when defeated by Audley Harrison in 2010

Les Clark

When the previous champion Albert Sosnowski had relinquished the crown in search of a world title challenge, Audley Harrison fought for the vacant European heavyweight title against fellow Briton Michael Sprott in Wood Green, London, on 9 April 2010.

Sprott, the former British and Commonwealth champion, had previously defeated Harrison on 17 February 2007 by a stoppage in round three when defending the European Union heavyweight title and contesting the vacant English heavyweight title. However, on this occasion, Harrison was able to gain revenge by knocking out Sprott in round twelve to win the crown.

This victory meant that Harrison then became just the third Olympic gold medallist to win the European heavyweight title (the previous two being Lennox Lewis in 1988 and Wladimir Klitschko in1996).

It's always good to see a boxer keeping active in the ring – something which Cuban heavyweight Mike Perez clearly believes in. The show, which took place on 15 May 2010 in Limerick, Ireland, saw Perez box twice in one night in bouts scheduled for four rounds. First opponent was Latvian Edgars Kalnars, who was stopped in the first round. Later that evening, Perez disposed of Tomas Mrazek of the Czech Republic when this bout was halted in the third round.

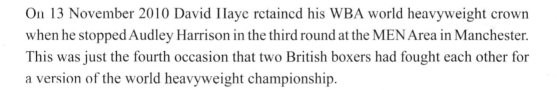

In a contest scheduled for twelve rounds for the vacant English heavyweight title and British heavyweight championship eliminator on 25 June 2010 in Brentwood, Essex, Tyson Fury regained the English crown when he stopped opponent John McDermott in nine rounds. For the first time in the history of the sport judges were used in an English title fight. The officials at this historic event were Howard Foster, Victor Loughlin and Richie Davies.

On 13 November 2010 David Haye retained his WBA world heavyweight crown when he stopped Audley Harrison in the third round at the MEN Area in Manchester. This was just the fourth occasion that two British boxers had fought each other for a version of the world heavyweight championship.

BRITONS WHO HAVE FOUGHT EACH OTHER

Winner	Opponent	Result	Date
Lennox Lewis (WBC champion)	Frank Bruno	Lewis retained title by way of a seven-round stoppage	1 Oct 1993
Henry Akinwande (WBO champion)	Scott Welch	Akinwande retained title by way of a twelve-round points decision	11 Jan 1997
Lennox Lewis (WBC champion)	Henry Akinwande	Lewis retained title by way of a five-round disqualification	12 Jul 1997

On 19 March 1994 Herbie Hide won the WBO world heavyweight crown when he knocked out holder Michael Bentt in round seven. Bentt was born in Britain, but was representing America, hence he is not included in the above list.

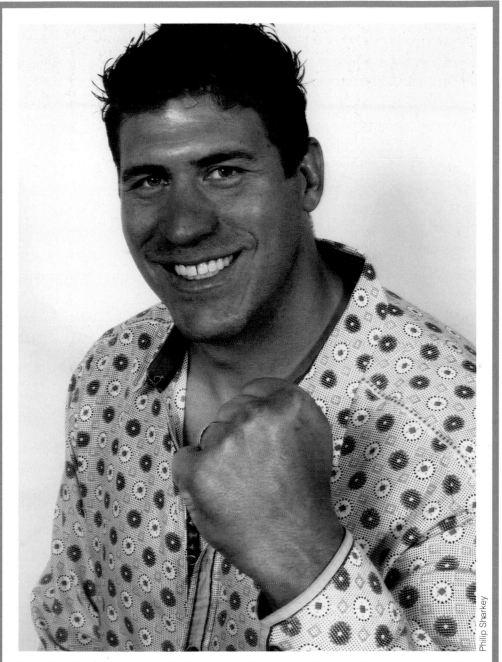

Philip Sharkey

Tye Fields of Canada was stopped in the first round in the final of the International heavyweight prize tournament by Cuban Mike Perez on 7 May 2011

193

Sir Henry Cooper, the former British, European and Commonwealth heavyweight champion, passed away on 1 May 2011. Henry, who was born on 3 May 1934, was without doubt one of the most popular boxers to emerge from Britain. He received an OBE in 1969 and was knighted in 2000.

Henry's left hook, known as 'Enery's 'ammer' kept the fans on the edge of their seats in anticipation wondering if or when it would land, since they knew that if the punch found the chin of his opponent it would probably end the contest.

Cooper won the ABA light-heavyweight crown in 1952 and 1953 and during his professional career crossed gloves with men like Muhammad Ali (twice), Floyd Patterson, Ingemar Johansson, Zora Folley (twice), Karl Mildenberger, Joe Erskine (five times), Joe Bugner, Jack Bodell (twice), Brian London (three times), Dick Richardson (twice), and Billy Walker.

Henry won the BBC's Sports Personality of the year award in 1967 and 1970, and was known fondly as 'Our 'Enery'.

Cuban Mike Perez represented Ireland to become the first man to win the International Heavyweight Prize-fighter tournament at Muswell Hill in London on 7 May 2011.

Earlier in the competition Perez had outpointed Kertson Manswell of Trinidad and Tobago over three rounds. In the semi-final he had stopped Grégory Tony of France in the first round. Then, in the final, Perez stopped Canadian Tye Fields in the first round.

It was the moment of truth for both Wladimir Klitschko of Ukraine, the reigning IBF, WBO and IBO world heavyweight title-holder, and Britain's WBA king David Haye. They met on 2 July 2011 in Hamburg, Germany. In a unification contest the two men faced each other to see who was the supreme fighter in the division. After twelve rounds Klitschko won the decision on points to add Haye's title to his collection.

Philip Sharkey

When Tyson Fury defeated Dereck Chisora in 2011, he became the tallest man, along with James Oyebola, to hold the British heavyweight crown

When Wladimir Klitschko defeated David Haye a unique situation occurred since the Klitschko family now held all the major world heavyweight titles, with Wladimir's older brother Vitali holding the WBC version of the championship.

On 23 July 2011 Tyson Fury outpointed defending champion Dereck Chisora over twelve rounds for the British and Commonwealth heavyweight titles at Wembley Area. In so doing Fury became joint holder with the late former champion James Oyebola (who reigned from 1994–5) as the tallest man to hold the British crown. The recorded height of both Fury and Oyebola is 6 ft 9 in.

After defeating David Haye to add the WBA version of the world heavyweight title to his collection of IBF, WBO and IBO championships, the WBA elevated Wladimir Klitschko to the status of 'super champion', making way for a category called Regular Heavyweight title. On 27 August 2011 in Erfurt, Germany, Alexander Povetkin outpointed the former WBA champion Ruslan Chagaev of Uzbekistan over twelve rounds for the vacant regular crown. Povetkin became the third Russian-born boxer to hold a version of the championship (previous holders being Nikolay Valuev and Sultan Ibragimov).

When Alexander Povetkin won the world title he became the tenth former Olympic Gold medallist to win a version of the world heavyweight championship. Povetkin won gold at Super-heavyweight in 2004. Previous gold medal winners were:

★ ★ ★ ★ ★ ★ ★ ★ ★ ★ ★ ★ ★ ★ ★ ★ ★ ★ ★

★★★★★ OLYMPIC GOLD MEDAL ★★★★★
WINNERS

BOXER	DIVISION	YEAR
Floyd Patterson	Middleweight	1952
Cassius Clay (later M. Ali)	Light-heavyweight	1960
Joe Frazier	Heavyweight	1964
George Foreman	Heavyweight	1968
Leon Spinks	Light-heavyweight	1976
Michael Spinks	Middleweight	1976
Ray Mercer	Heavyweight	1988
Lennox Lewis	Super-heavyweight	1988
Wladimir Klitschko	Super-heavyweight	1996

On 10 September 2011, Poland staged its first world heavyweight title contest. In Wroclaw, in western Poland, the champion Vitali Klitschko of Ukraine defended his WBC crown against Tomasz Adamek, the former WBC world light-heavyweight champion and IBF cruiserweight title-holder. Despite home advantage, Adamek was unable to win a third world crown and was stopped by Klitschko in round ten.

Former world heavyweight champion Joe Frazier passed away at the age of sixty-seven on 7 November 2011. Born on 12 January 1944, Frazier fought a host of quality fighters like Muhammad Ali (three times), George Foreman (twice), Jimmy Ellis (twice), Oscar Bonavena, Jerry Quarry (twice), Eddie Machen, George Chuvalo, Bob Foster, Buster Mathis, and Joe Bugner.

Finland saw its first world heavyweight title fight on 3 December 2011 when Russia's Alexander Povetkin knocked out American challenger Cedric Boswell in round eight in defence of his regular WBA crown. The contest took place in Helsinki.

On the Povetkin–Boswell promotion, Robert Helenius became the first Finnish boxer to hold the European heavyweight championship when he outpointed former British and Commonwealth heavyweight king Dereck Chisora over twelve rounds for the vacant title. Helenius was also defending his WBA and WBO Intercontinental heavyweight titles.

It could be said that the contest between David Price and John McDermott for the vacant English heavyweight title, which took place on 21 January 2012, was fast and furious. Price knocked out former champion McDermott in seventy-three seconds of the first round in Liverpool. This was the first time that this particular championship had been won in the opening session.

On 14 April 2012 former British, Commonwealth and English heavyweight champion Tyson Fury won the vacant Irish title at the Odyssey Area, stopping his opponent, former Commonwealth king, Martin Rogan, in round five. The contest produced something of a surprise in that Fury, who boxes orthodox, switched to southpaw for the duration of the fight.

On 5 May 2012 in Erfurt, Germany, Kubrat Pulev extended his undefeated record to sixteen when he captured the vacant European heavyweight championship by knocking out former holder Alexander Dimitrenko in round eleven. In so doing, Pulev became the first Bulgarian boxer to hold this title. (Pulev also made a successful defence of his IBF International title, which was also at stake.)

On 19 May 2012 David Price won the vacant British and Commonwealth heavy-weight titles, which had been relinquished by Tyson Fury, when he knocked out former Commonwealth champion Sam Sexton in the fourth round in Liverpool. In so doing he became the second boxer with an Olympic medal to capture the British crown. Price had won a bronze medal in the Super-heavyweight division in the 2008 Olympic Games, which had been held in Beijing. (Lennox Lewis, who had won a gold medal at the 1988 Olympic Games in Seoul at Super-heavyweight was the first to do so, winning the British heavyweight title on 6 March 1991.) Price also became the first boxer from Liverpool to win the British and Commonwealth heavyweight titles.

A controversial contest took place on 14 July 2012 when David Haye and Dereck Chisora crossed gloves in a well-documented grudge match in London. Haye fought his way to victory, stopping his opponent in round five in a contest which had been licensed by the Luxembourg Boxing Federation and not The British Boxing Board of Control. The vacant WBO International heavyweight title and the vacant WBA Inter-Continental heavyweight crown was at stake during the contest.

On 13 October 2012 two boxers climbed into the ring in Liverpool to contest the British and Commonwealth heavyweight titles. It was the first time that two Olympic medallists had fought each other for these titles. Champion David Price had won bronze at Super-heavyweight at the 2008 Beijing Games and challenger Audley Harrison had won gold in the same weight division at the Sydney Games in 2000. On this occasion bronze topped gold when Price retained the titles, stopping Harrison in eighty-two seconds of the first round.

On 30 November 2012 Andrew 'Freddie' Flintoff made his professional boxing debut, outpointing American Richard Dawson over four rounds in Manchester. Flintoff was a former cricketer who had previously played for Lancashire and England.

In Montreal, Canada, Britain's Hughie Fury made his professional debut a quick one, stopping his Canadian opponent David Whittom in the second round on 22 March 2013. Hughie is the cousin of Tyson Fury.

Former British and Commonwealth heavyweight champion Tyson Fury made his USA debut against former two-time IBF world cruiserweight title-holder Steve Cunningham of the USA at Madison Square Garden Theatre in New York. The bout, which took place on 20 April 2013, was an IBF eliminator for the world heavyweight title. Tyson's American debut proved successful when he extended his undefeated record to twenty-one, knocking out Cunningham in round seven to give him his best international victory at that time.

Leon Spinks III extended his undefeated professional record to four victories and one draw in a contest made a lightweight when he stopped Mexican opponent Enrique Guzman on 1 May 2013 in round one in Tijuana, Mexico. Spinks is the grandson of former world heavyweight champion Leon Spinks.

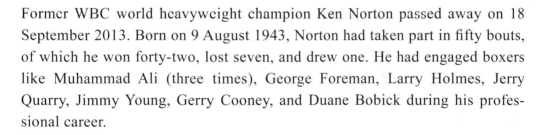

On 25 July 2013 Kyotaro Fujimoto won the vacant Japanese heavyweight title when he stopped opponent Okello Peter in round six in Tokyo. This was the first championship at the weight since 4 May 1957.

Former WBC world heavyweight champion Ken Norton passed away on 18 September 2013. Born on 9 August 1943, Norton had taken part in fifty bouts, of which he won forty-two, lost seven, and drew one. He had engaged boxers like Muhammad Ali (three times), George Foreman, Larry Holmes, Jerry Quarry, Jimmy Young, Gerry Cooney, and Duane Bobick during his professional career.

Ken Norton (here pictured in later years) shocked the boxing world when he outpointed Muhammad Ali over twelve rounds in March 1973

At the 2012 London Olympics, all eyes were on the exciting new prospect Anthony Joshua, who won a gold medal at Super-heavyweight. Anthony made his professional debut on 5 October 2013, knocking out his opponent Emanuele Leo in the first round in Greenwich, London.

Lucas Browne of Australia won the vacant Commonwealth heavyweight title on 26 April 2014 when he knocked out Canada's Eric Martel Bahoeli in round five in Sheffield, England. (David Price had relinquished said crown.) In so doing, Browne became the first non-Briton to hold this crown since Trevor Berbick of Canada, who reigned from 1981 to 1986.

In the same bout Browne also won the vacant WBC Eurasian Pacific Boxing Council heavyweight title.

Jimmy Ellis, the former WBA world heavyweight champion, passed away on 6 May 2014. He had been born on 24 February 1940. During his career, Jimmy took part in fifty-three contests, winning forty and losing twelve, with just one drawn. He crossed gloves with quality fighters like Leotis Martin, Oscar Bonavena, Jerry Quarry, Floyd Patterson, Joe Frazier (twice), George Chuvalo, Muhammad Ali, Earnie Shavers, Ron Lyle, and Joe Bugner.

In Los Angles on 10 May 2014, Bermane Stiverne won the vacant WBC world heavyweight title when he stopped American opponent Chris Arreola in round six following the retirement of Vitali Klitschko. In so doing Stiverne became the third boxer from Canada following Tommy Burns and Trevor Berbick and the first Haitian to win this crown.

BOXERS' NICKNAMES

BOXER	NICKNAME
Muhammad Ali	The Louisville Lip/The Greatest
Max Baer	Livermore Larruper/Madcap Maxie
Riddick Bowe	Big Daddy
James J. Braddock	The Cinderella Man
Lamon Brewster	Relentless
Shannon Brigg	The Cannon
Tommy Burns	The Little Giant of Hanover
Chris Byrd	Rapid Fire
Primo Carnera	The Ambling Alp
Ruslan Chagaev	White Tyson
Ezzard Charles	The Cincinnati Cobra
James J. Corbett	Gentleman Jim
Jack Dempsey	The Manassa Mauler
Michael Dokes	Dynamite
James Douglas	Buster
Bob Fitzsimmons	Freckled Bob/Ruby Robert
Joe Frazier	Smokin' Joe
Marvin Hart	The Fighting Kentuckian
David Haye	'Hayemaker'
Herbie Hide	The Dancing Destroyer
Larry Holmes	The Easton Assassin
Evander Holyfield	The Real Deal
Sultan Ibragimov	The Russian Bomber
James J. Jeffries	The Boilermaker
Jack Johnson	Little Artha/Galvestone Giant
Vitali Klitschko	Dr Iron Fist
Wladimir Klitschko	Dr Steel Hammer

★ ★

MANY WORLD HEAVYWEIGHT CHAMPIONS HAVE ACQUIRED A NICKNAME DURING THEIR RESPECTIVE CAREERS

BOXER	NICKNAME
Lennox Lewis	The Lion
Siarhei Liakhovich	White Wolfe
Joe Louis	Brown Bomber
Oliver McCall	The Atomic Bull
Rocky Marciano	The Brockton Blockbuster
Oleg Maskaev	The Big O
Ray Mercer	Merciless
Tommy Morrison	The Duke
Samuel Peter	The Nigerian Nightmare
Hasim Rahman	The Rock
John Ruiz	The Quiet Man
Corrie Sanders	The Sniper
Max Schmeling	Black Uhlan
Bruce Seldon	The Atlantic City Express
Jack Sharkey	Boston Gob
James Smith	Bonecrusher
Leon Spinks	Neon Leon
John L. Sullivan	Boston Strongboy
Pinklon Thomas	Pink
Tony Tubbs	TNT
Tony Tucker	TNT
Gene Tunney	The Fighting Marine
Mike Tyson	Iron Mike
Nikolay Valuev	Beast from the East
Mike Weaver	Hercules
Jess Willard	Pottawatomie Giant
Tim Witherspoon	Terrible Tim

★ ★

Index